Charlie Brown's Fifth Super Book of Questions and Answers

...about all kinds of things
and how they work!

Charlie Brown's Fifth Super Book of Questions and Answers

...about all kinds of things and how they work!

Based on the Charles M. Schulz Characters

Random House New York

Editor: Hedda Nussbaum

Art Director: Eleanor Ehrhardt
Designer: Terry Flanagan
Layout: Charlotte Staub
Picture Research: Anne Christensen

Production: Edward McGill, Elaine Silber

Special thanks to:

Dr. Ira Freeman
Science Consultant,
Former Professor of Physics
Rutgers University

Photograph and illustration credits: American Telephone & Telegraph Company, 123, 126, 132; American Petroleum Institute, 11; Association of American Railroads, 95; Bell Laboratories, 68, 125, 126; Bergen Record, 34, 35; The Bettman Archive, Inc., 46, 61; Black Star/© 1979 Ricardo Ferro, 38; Consumer & Educational Affairs Dept., Coats & Clark Inc., 44; Colonial Williamsburg Photograph, 28; Consolidated Edison Company of New York, Inc., 102; © 1979 The Cousteau Society, 83; Culver Pictures, Inc., 33; Terry Flanagan, 17; Rita Ford Music Boxes, New York, 20; Ford Motor Company, 47; © Four By Five, 95; © Fundamental Photographs, 20, 57, 69, 82, 99, 114, 141; Honeywell, Inc., 74; Lares Manufacturing Co., Inc., 10; Richard Megna/Fundamental Photographs, 14; Richard Megna/Fundamental Photographs © 1980, 4, 56; Richard Megna/Fundamental Photographs © 1981, 71; The Metropolitan Museum of Art, Gift of Mary J. Kingsland, 1906, 22; The Metropolitan Museum of Art, Gift of I. N. Phelps Stokes, Edward S. Hawes, Alice Mary Hawes, Marion Augusta Hawes, 1937, 43; The Metropolitan Museum of Art, Gift of Mrs. Henry McSweeney, 1959, 51; The Metropolitan Museum of Art, Gift of Mrs. John H. Lufbery and Shirley Sammis Foulds, 1978, 52; The Metropolitan Museum of Art, The Crosby Brown Collection of Musical Instruments, 1889, 54; The Metropolitan Museum of Art, The Crosby Brown Collection of Musical Instruments, 1889, and Gift of the University Museum, University of Pennsylvania, 1953, 55; Museum of Modern Art/Film Stills Archive, 65; National Oceanic & Atmospheric Administration, 85; New Hampshire Ball Bearings, Inc., 13; Nova Scotia Department of Government Services Information Services Photo, 48; Otis Elevator Company, 40; Kip Peticolas/Fundamental Photographs © 1980, 37; Ray-O-Vac, a Corporation of INCO Electro-Energy, 103; Scientific Atlanta, 131; The Singer Company, 42, 43; Smithsonian Institution Photo No. 46838, 87; Smithsonian Institution Photo No. Edison 51144, 116; Stanley Tools, Division of the Stanley Works, 9; Tennessee Valley Authority, 107; Yale University Art Gallery, Gift of George Hoadly, Yale 1801, 46.

Library of Congress Cataloging in Publication Data

Schulz, Charles M. Charlie Brown's fifth super book of questions and answers. Includes index. SUMMARY: Charlie Brown and the rest of the Peanuts gang help present a host of facts about a wide variety of simple and complex machines in question and answer format. 1. Machinery—Juvenile literature. 2. Machinery—Miscellanea—Juvenile literature. [1. Machinery—Miscellanea. 2. Questions and answers] I. Title. II. Title: Fifth super book of questions and answers.
TJ147.S43   600   79-28441
ISBN 0-394-84355-X trade   ISBN 0-394-94355-4 lib. bdg.
Manufactured in the United States of America   1 2 3 4 5 6 7 8 9 0

Introduction

Two hundred years ago, people had very few machines to make their lives easier. Today, everywhere you look are wonderful inventions—from can openers and light bulbs to lasers and color television. Have you ever wondered how these things work, and who invented them? If so, you've come to the right book. Here you will find answers to questions like "How does a picture get to your television set?" "What makes a ball-point pen write?" "Who invented the radio?" "What is solar heating?" "How does a laser work?" "What makes toasters and electric irons get hot?" And many, many more.

And once again, Charlie Brown, Snoopy, Lucy, Sally, Peppermint Patty, Linus, Woodstock, and the rest of the Peanuts gang are here to help out with the questions. So you can have fun while you find out the answers!

Contents

Machines and How They Work

What is a machine?

A machine is an object that makes hard work easier or slow work faster. It gives the person using it greater speed or greater force. ("Force" means a push or pull.) A machine is usually made up of a few connected parts. A vacuum cleaner is a machine that makes housecleaning easy and fast. A car is a machine that lets people move much faster than they could by walking. A telephone is a machine that makes it possible to talk to someone far away.

Do all machines have motors?

No. There are many machines that have no motors. The power for doing work with many of these machines comes from people's muscles. A scissors, a shovel, a saw, a broom, a screwdriver, a corkscrew, a bottle opener, and even a fly swatter are machines without motors. And so is a seesaw.

How can a seesaw be a machine?

A seesaw is a machine because it helps to do work—the work of lifting another person. In fact, with a seesaw, you can lift a person heavier than you are (if the heavier person moves forward on the seesaw). You certainly couldn't do that without the help of a machine! The seesaw makes it possible for you to use greater force than you could without it.

A seesaw is a kind of machine called a lever (LEV-ur). A lever is a stiff bar that turns on a point. This point is called a fulcrum (FULL-krum). When a seesaw is used by two people who weigh about the same, its fulcrum is right around the center of the bar.

2

What other machine can you find in a playground?

A slide. A slide is a kind of machine called an inclined plane. A plane is a flat surface. An incline is a slope or tilt. An inclined plane is a tilted flat surface. It makes moving things between high places and low places easier. On a slide, the thing that moves down easily is you!

An inclined plane something like a slide is used to unload boxes from a truck. Often this machine has little wheels on it. The wheels make the boxes move more quickly down the tilted plane.

Airplanes got their name from the planes, or flat surfaces, that hold them up in the air. These flat surfaces are the wings!

Who invented the wheel?

Nobody knows. But it was one of the most useful inventions ever made.

How are wheels used?

Wheels help people and things move around on land. Cars and trains could not work if they didn't have wheels on which to move. Neither could bicycles, skateboards, shopping carts, baby carriages, and lots of other things. Wheels sometimes connect motors to machines. In this way motors, rather than people, can supply the energy to make the machines work. Some machines that use wheels are a doorknob, a water faucet, an eggbeater, and a drill.

latch

axle

How does a doorknob work?

A doorknob is a wheel attached to a rod called an axle. The axle goes through the door. At the other end of the axle is another doorknob. When you turn one of the doorknobs, it turns the axle. The axle pushes a bar that's connected to the latch. The latch is the piece of metal that sticks out of the edge of the door. It fits into a little hole in the wall when the door is closed. The latch is what keeps the door from opening until you turn the knob. When you close the door, a spring makes the latch pop into the hole in the wall. The same spring also does another job. It makes the doorknob go back into place after you turn the knob and let go.

CLOMP!

WHY HE NEEDS AN AUTOMATIC DOOR-OPENER IS BEYOND ME

How does a faucet work?

A faucet is attached to the end of a water pipe. It holds the water in the pipe until you decide to let some out. There is a hole between the water pipe and the spigot. This hole is stopped up by a plug. Turning the handle in one direction causes the plug to come partway out of the hole. Then water flows through. Turning the handle in the other direction puts the plug back in the hole. Then water can't leave the pipe. At the end of the plug is a piece of rubber called a washer. It makes the plug fit tightly in the hole. So the faucet doesn't drip when you turn it off.

The ancient Romans were using
water faucets about 2,000 years ago!

Is a crank a grouchy person?

Yes. But the word "crank" has another meaning, too. On a machine, a crank is a bar or handle that you turn in order to make a wheel or axle turn. When the wheel or axle turns, the machine works. The pedals on a bicycle are cranks. When you pedal, the wheels turn and the bike moves. The handle you turn to make a car window go up and down also is a crank. So is the handle you turn on a fishing reel.

Why do people use a rod and reel for fishing?

To get their bait into deep water where the big fish are. When you fish from the edge of a lake or river, or from an ocean beach, you are far from the deep water. You need a fishing rod to help you throw your fishing line farther than your arm could alone. You also need a very long line. The reel stores the long line neatly and it keeps it from getting tangled. When you throw (or "cast," as fishermen say), the reel lets the line go out very far. When you catch a fish, the crank on the reel helps you to pull in the line quickly and easily.

Why is an eggbeater better than a fork for whipping cream?

You can whip cream faster with an eggbeater than you can with a fork. An eggbeater has a crank. When you turn the crank, it turns a gear. This gear is a wheel with little teeth on it. It pushes two smaller gears that are attached to the two beaters. As these three gears turn, their teeth hook onto each other and then unhook again. Each time the big gear goes around once, the little gears go around a few times. So do the beaters. This means the little gears are turning faster than the big gear. It also means that the beaters are spinning faster than you are turning the crank. An eggbeater helps you by changing slow cranking into fast beating.

What machine looks like an eggbeater?

One kind of hand drill. It has a crank and gears like an eggbeater. But instead of beaters, it has a chuck and a bit. The bit is the part of the drill that actually makes the holes. Some bits look a lot like wood screws. The chuck holds the bit in place.

When someone wants to drill a hole in wood, metal, or plastic, here is what must be done. The person drilling holds the bit against the proper spot and turns the handle. The handle turns the gears. The gears turn the chuck and the bit, creating a hole.

Hand drill

chuck

bit

9

Does a dentist's drill work like other kinds of drills?

A dentist's drill is really more like a file than like other drills. Dental drill bits are called burs. A bur is a tiny, rough ball on the end of a stick. When the bur spins around, it scrapes away little pieces of tooth. Years ago, dentists used drills that turned very slowly. That meant it took a long time to drill a cavity. And nobody likes to have his or her teeth drilled for a long time. Modern dentists use drills that spin the bur many thousands of times a minute. That's fast! And it means the dentist can finish drilling in a very short time. But such fast scraping against the tooth makes the drill and the tooth get hot. So they are cooled by water. It flows through holes in the drill onto the patient's tooth.

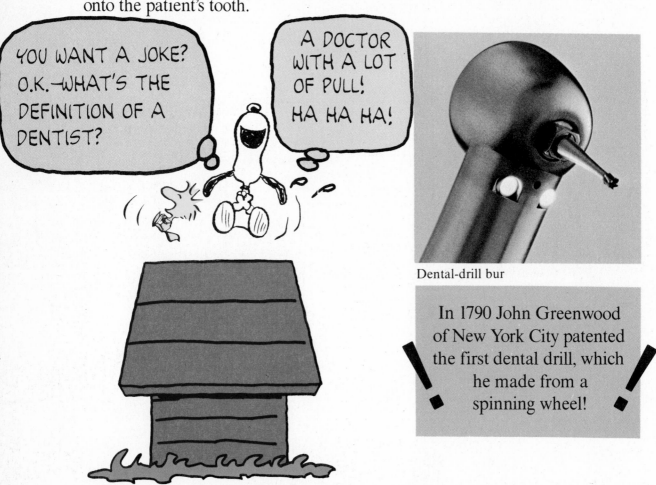

Dental-drill bur

In 1790 John Greenwood of New York City patented the first dental drill, which he made from a spinning wheel!

What do inventors do to machines when they patent them?

When inventors patent their machines, they get exclusive rights from their government to make and sell the machines. This means that no one is allowed to copy their machines. And no one else is allowed to make money from their ideas. In the United States of America, a patent lasts for 17 years. It cannot be renewed.

How are oil wells drilled?

Oil-well drills have to cut through rock to reach an underground pool of oil. Rock is very hard to cut. And often the hole has to be miles deep. Scraping on rock makes most drill bits wear out quickly and get dull. So, a special oil-well bit was designed to break the rock into little pieces. The bit has toothed wheels that look much like gears. The teeth are made of hardened metal. And sometimes they are diamond tipped for extra hardness. When the bit turns, the wheels roll around. The teeth strike the rock like dozens of hammers.

The bit is attached to one end of a metal pipe. A motor at the top of the drilling hole makes the pipe spin around. A metal tower, called a derrick, is over the drilling hole. The derrick holds the pipe upright and lets it down into the hole.

Oil-drill bit

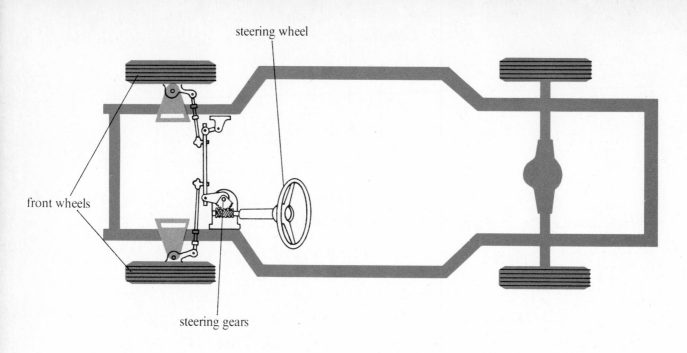

steering wheel

front wheels

steering gears

How does a steering wheel make a car turn?

A steering wheel is connected to a long metal bar, like an axle. It extends down into a metal gearbox in the front of the car. When you turn the steering wheel, you make the bar turn a gear. In many cars the gear is a worm gear. The worm gear turns another gear, which is connected to a lever. The lever is connected to two rods. One rod is attached to the left front wheel, and the other is attached to the right front wheel. When you turn the steering wheel, the gears move the lever. The rods attached to the lever make the car's front wheels turn left or right.

Question:
How does a steering
wheel make a car
turn?
Answer:
How should I know!
Sally Brown

What makes roller skates and skateboards roll easily?

Inside the wheels of roller skates and skateboards are little steel balls called ball bearings. The ball bearings fit into grooves between the wheels and the axles. If there were no ball bearings, the wheels would rub and scrape on the axles. This kind of rubbing and scraping is called friction (FRICK-shun). It makes wheels hard to turn. If wheels are hard to turn, they can't roll fast. Ball bearings reduce friction and make wheels easy to turn. You can reduce friction even more if you squirt a drop of oil on the ball bearings. Bicycles, cars, and many other kinds of machines use bearings and oil or grease to make them run better.

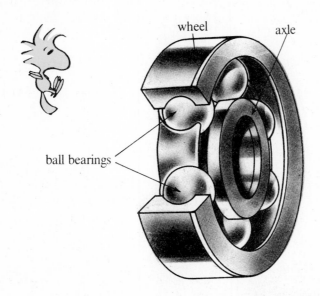

wheel axle

ball bearings

JOE SKATEBOARD!

13

How do the gears on a one-speed bicycle work?

A one-speed bike has just two gears. They are called sprockets. One sprocket is attached to the pedals and one is attached to the rear wheel. A loop of chain goes around the two sprockets. When you pedal, you turn the pedal sprocket. It pushes the chain, which turns the rear-wheel sprocket. And that turns the wheel to make the bike go.

Why do some bicycles have ten speeds?

So that the rider can make the bike go fast without pedaling fast. And so that the rider can go up a hill without straining too hard. When you ride a one-speed bike, some hills are too hard to ride up. You have to get off and push the bike. If you want to go fast on a one-speed bike, you have to pedal very, very fast. And you soon get tired. Three-speed bicycles are better for climbing hills or going fast because they have more gears than one-speed bicycles. More gears mean more possible speeds. Ten-speed bikes are even better.

14

How do the gears on a ten-speed bicycle work?

A ten-speed bike has seven sprockets. Two are attached to the pedals and five are attached to the rear wheel. Each sprocket is a different size. The chain is always looped around one of the pedal sprockets and one of the rear-wheel sprockets. The bike has controls that let you move the chain from one sprocket to another. By doing this, you can get more speed or more forward force—but not both at the same time.

If you wanted to go fast on flat ground, you would put your chain around the large pedal sprocket and the smallest rear-wheel sprocket. This combination would give you the most speed, but the least forward force. You don't need much force to move on flat ground.

If you wanted to go up a hill without pedaling hard, you would need a lot of forward force. So you would put your chain around the small pedal sprocket and the largest rear-wheel sprocket. This combination would give you the most forward force but the least speed. You would go up the hill easily, but slowly.

Ten combinations of rear-wheel and pedal sprockets are possible. That is why the bicycle is called a ten-speed bike. After you have ridden a ten-speed bike for a while, you get to know which combinations are best for the kind of riding you are doing.

What makes springs bouncy?

Springs are bouncy because they have elasticity (ee-lass-TISS-ih-tee). This means you can stretch them or bend them or squeeze them, and they will quickly go back to their original shape when you let go. Rubber bands have elasticity. That's why people often call them elastic bands.

How does a pogo stick help people to jump high?

A pogo stick has a spring inside it. A spring, or any elastic thing, can store energy. When you jump down on a pogo stick, you use energy to squeeze the spring. The spring stores the energy for just a moment, until you start to jump up. Then, the energy in the spring is let out. It gives you an extra boost and helps you to go higher.

! In 1976 William Hanrahan kept jumping on a pogo stick for ten hours and one minute. He made 70,076 jumps! !

THAT'S THE WAY!

Is a diving board a machine?

Yes, a diving board is really a spring. Springs aren't always shaped like a curly piece of wire. Springs can be flat, and they can even be made of wood. Anything that bends without breaking and then snaps back to its original position is a spring. Divers like a springy diving board because it helps them to jump high. When divers jump high, they have time to do fancy tricks in the air before they plunge into the water.

How do a bow and arrow work?

The bow is a spring. When you pull back the string, you bend the bow and put energy into it. When you let go of the string, the energy is let out very suddenly. It gives the arrow a strong, fast push.

An arrow is not very heavy. You could throw it with your hand, as if it were a spear. But it wouldn't go very far. This is because your hand can't push the arrow as fast as the bow does. The faster you push the arrow, the farther it will go.

 Some very strong bows can shoot an arrow more than half a mile (nearly 1 kilometer)!

How does a bathroom scale work?

A bathroom scale uses a spring to measure weight. When you stand on the scale, you cause a bar to pull down on the spring. The spring stretches. The heavier you are, the more it stretches. As the spring stretches, a piece of metal swings down and pushes a second bar. This bar is long and flat and has gear teeth along one edge. It turns a small gear. The small gear turns an axle, which turns a wheel. The wheel has numbers printed on it. These are the numbers that show through the window in the top of the scale. When the wheel stops turning, you see a number under the pointer. This is how much you weigh.

Do all scales have springs?

No. Doctors and nurses weigh people on scales that have no springs. This kind of scale uses a lever to measure weight. The lever works like a seesaw. When you step on the scale, the weight of your body pulls down one side of the lever. The other side of the lever has metal weights. These can slide along bars that have numbers. The doctor or nurse moves the metal weights back and forth along the bars until the lever balances. If a person weighs 82 pounds, for example, the lever will balance when the big weight is on 50 and the small weight is on 32 (50+32=82). Doctors and nurses prefer this kind of scale because it is more exact than a bathroom scale.

METAL WEIGHTS

LEVER

spring

roller

gears

reeds

Simple music-box mechanism

CARE TO MINUET, BEAUTIFUL?

Music box with extra rollers stored underneath

What makes a music box play when you wind it up?

A music box is powered by a spring that works like a motor. This kind of spring is a flat piece of metal rolled up like a spool of ribbon. When you wind up the spring, you are rolling it tight. You are also putting energy into it. When the spring is released, the energy stored in it makes it unwind and turn around in a circle. When the spring turns around, it turns a gear. This gear turns a second gear, which is attached to a roller. The roller has little spikes sticking out of it. When the roller turns, the spikes push aside thin pieces of metal called reeds. The reeds twang like strings of a guitar. And you hear music.

20

Why does a windup watch tick?

Because it keeps stopping and starting again. A windup watch is powered by the same kind of spring that runs a music box. The spring turns gears, which make the hands go around. If the gears kept turning, without ever stopping, the energy in the spring would escape very fast. And the hands would whirl around too quickly. So something called an escapement (eh-SCAPE-ment) was invented to keep the hands from spinning too fast. Here's how it works.

Inside the watch is a tiny lever. At each end of the lever is a hook. The lever flips back and forth like a seesaw going up and down. Each time the lever flips, one of the hooks catches a tooth on one of the watch's gears. The watch stops for a fraction of a second. Then the hook releases the gear tooth and the watch starts again. Stop and go, stop and go. Tick, tick, tick, tick. Each tick is the sound of a hook letting go of a gear tooth.

 You can *see* your watch stopping and starting.
Just keep your eye on the jerky motion of the second hand!

Why is a grandfather clock tall?

A grandfather clock is tall because it needs a lot of room inside for the long clock parts that hang down. Most grandfather clocks have a glass door in the front. You can look in and see the parts—weights, chimes, and a pendulum.

What is a pendulum?

A pendulum is the clock part you see swinging back and forth. It controls how fast the clock runs, just like the escapement in a windup watch. You can make the pendulum longer or shorter. Just loosen a screw and move the pendulum up or down. If you make it longer, the clock will run slower. If you make it shorter, the clock will run faster.

Why do grandfather clocks have to be wound up?

Unless they are wound, they run out of energy. Some clocks have a windup spring—just as a watch does. But grandfather clocks have no windup spring. They get their energy from the weights that hang down behind the pendulum. Each weight pulls on the chain. The chains turn gears inside the top of the clock. As the clock runs, the weights move slowly down. After a while, the weights have to be pulled up again, or else the clock will stop. Winding the clock lifts the weights.

What makes a grandfather clock chime?

Hanging behind the weights on a clock are metal tubes called chimes. They make musical sounds when small hammers in the top of the clock hit them. The gears that turn the clock's hands also make the hammers strike the chimes. Every hour, on the hour, the chimes play a short tune: one bong at one o'clock, two at two o'clock, and all the way up to twelve bongs at noon or midnight.

Grandfathers aren't the only ones who have a clock named after them. Grandmothers do too! A grandmother clock looks just like a grandfather clock, only it's shorter.

What makes an alarm clock ring?

A bell. Some clocks have the bell on top of the case. Others have it inside. With many clocks, the metal case itself is the bell. The bell rings when a small hammer or clapper strikes it. The hammer is held down by a hook until the right time comes.

Suppose you set your clock for 7:30. Behind the knob you use to set the alarm is a gear. On it is a special trigger bump. At 7:30 this bump will meet up with a hole in the gear that turns the hour hand. When the bump goes into the hole, the hour-hand gear moves closer to the alarm gear. This movement causes the hook holding the hammer to be pushed out of place. The hammer is released. And . . . Rrrrrriiiiinnnggg! When you shut off the alarm, a hook will hold the hammer still once again.

hook

bell

alarm gear

hammer

hour hand gear

How does a toaster know when to pop up?

Inside a toaster is a timer, which is just like a clock. When you push the knob down to start the toaster, you are also winding up the timer. The timer goes ticka-ticka-tick while it's unwinding. When the timer is all unwound, it releases a spring that makes your toast pop up. If you set your toaster to make light toast, then the timer will run fast. If you set it to make dark toast, then the timer will run slowly. Your toast will stay down inside and cook longer. The timer on most toasters works even when the toaster is not plugged in. It does not need electricity to do its job.

I'LL TAKE MY TOAST WITH LOTS OF GRAPE JELLY, PLEASE....

SIGH

THAT'S LIFE... YOU SET YOUR ALARM FOR SIX O'CLOCK, AND THE WORM SETS HIS FOR FIVE-THIRTY

How does a key unlock a lock?

Inside a lock are little metal rods called tumblers. Most locks have five tumblers. They are lined up in a row in the top part of the lock. The tumblers poke down into the part of the lock that turns. In this way, they jam the lock so that it can't turn. Suppose you put the right key into a lock. The bumps on the top of the key push the tumblers out of the way. Then you can turn the key and unlock the lock. But suppose you use the wrong key. It will push the tumblers too far or not enough. This is because the bumps on a wrong key are higher or lower than the bumps on the right key. If you use the wrong key, the tumblers will keep jamming the lock so that it won't open.

WOODSTOCK IS RIGHT. IF YOU LIVE IN A NEST YOU DON'T HAVE TO BOTHER ABOUT LOCKS....

tumbler

key

Why was the carpet sweeper invented?

Because of an allergy. Mr. Melville R. Bissell owned a china shop. Unfortunately, he was allergic to straw dust. All the china that arrived at his shop came packed in dusty straw. After he unpacked a shipment of china, he needed to get the dust out of his shop. Otherwise his allergy would bother him. This was back around 1876, before vacuum cleaners were invented. With no vacuum cleaner available, Bissell had to use a broom. But brooms kick dust into the air. For a person who is allergic, straw dust in the air is even worse than straw dust on the floor. So Bissell invented a sweeper with a built-in dustpan. When he cleaned with it, the dust went right into the pan. It never went into the air. Bissell sweepers soon became popular in many parts of the world. They are still used today.

Why does a saw make sawdust?

Because a saw works like hundreds of very tiny axes chopping. An ax strikes with great force. It bites big chunks out of a piece of wood. A saw is for making careful, neat cuts in wood, plastic, or metal. Each tooth on a saw blade is like a tiny, sharp ax. When you make a saw go back and forth across what you are cutting, the teeth bite off little chunks. Each little chunk is a piece of sawdust.

! The sharpest saws have teeth made of diamonds! !

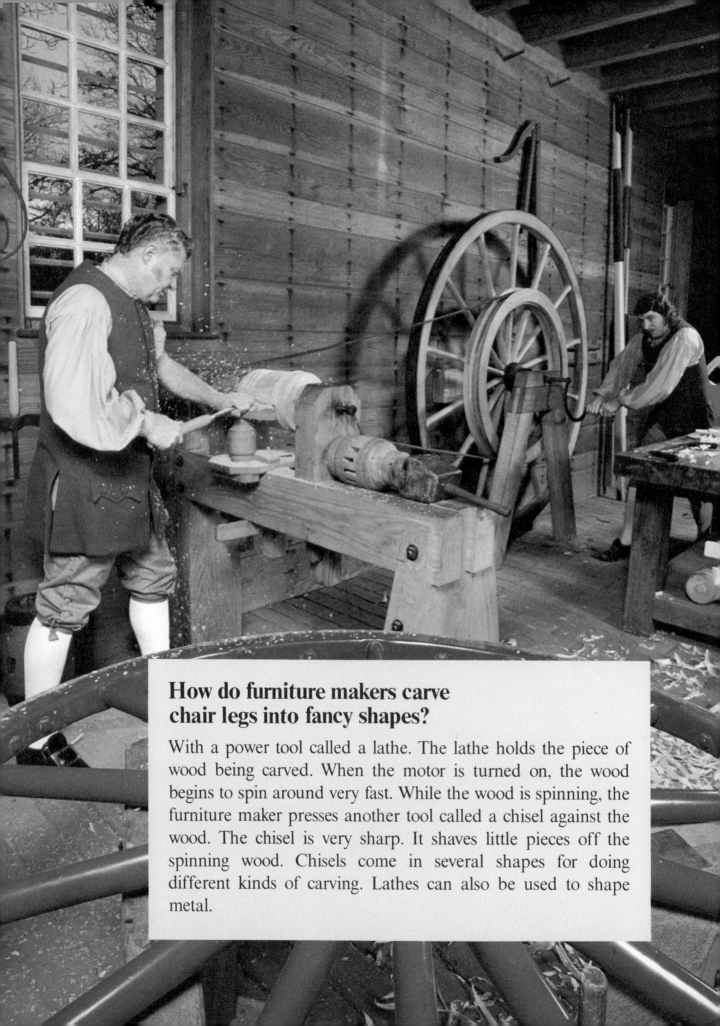

How do furniture makers carve chair legs into fancy shapes?

With a power tool called a lathe. The lathe holds the piece of wood being carved. When the motor is turned on, the wood begins to spin around very fast. While the wood is spinning, the furniture maker presses another tool called a chisel against the wood. The chisel is very sharp. It shaves little pieces off the spinning wood. Chisels come in several shapes for doing different kinds of carving. Lathes can also be used to shape metal.

Why do sharp knives cut better than dull knives?

Because sharp knife blades are thinner than dull knife blades. And because sharp knife blades have a rougher edge than dull knife blades. In order to cut through something tough, such as the skin of a tomato, you need a sharp knife. Tiny teeth, so small you can see them only under a microscope, are all along the edge of a sharp blade (unless it's the blade of a steak knife—then it has large teeth). These teeth bite and tear at the tomato skin. And, because a sharp blade is very thin, it has a very narrow area of tomato skin to push through. The dull blade is wider than a sharp blade. So it has to push through more tomato skin. It also has no little teeth for biting into the skin. So a dull blade can cut only soft things like butter or a slice of white bread.

How does a lawn mower cut grass?

With a blade. The most popular type of lawn mower is the rotary power mower. "Rotary" means turning or spinning around. A rotary blade spins like a fan or an airplane propeller. A gasoline or electric motor supplies the energy to spin the blade. When the blade spins, it creates a wind. The spinning blade pulls air up from underneath the mower. It blows the air out a hole in the side or the back of the mower. The moving air makes the grass stand up straight. Then the blade can chop it all off at the same height. The result is a lawn that looks smooth and even.

Does a lawn mower do anything besides cut grass?

Yes. The air pulled in from underneath the mower sucks up leaves. It also sucks up any paper or trash that might be lying around. The blade chops the leaves and trash into tiny pieces. Some mowers collect the grass clippings, leaves, and trash in a bag. Then you can easily throw them away. Other mowers blow all the chopped-up pieces out onto the lawn. Then you have to rake them up.

The biggest lawn mower on record is 60 feet (18 meters) wide. It can mow one acre (less than one hectare) of grass in one minute!

How does a pencil sharpener sharpen pencils?

Inside a hand-cranked sharpener, there are two metal rollers side by side. Sharp ridges, almost like knife blades, stick out from the rollers. These ridges are for shaving little pieces of wood off a pencil. The pencil fits into a space between the two rollers. The space is wide at one end. It comes to a point at the other end. When you turn the crank, the rollers spin. They shave your pencil into the same shape as the space between the two rollers.

How does an electric pencil sharpener work?

Instead of a hand crank, an electric pencil sharpener has a motor. But the rollers that shave the pencil are the same in the electric as in the manual sharpener. When you poke your pencil into the hole of an electric pencil sharpener, the pencil pushes a lever. The lever flips a switch that turns the motor on. The motor makes the rollers spin to sharpen the pencil.

The "lead" (led) inside a pencil isn't really made of lead. It's mostly a soft, black mineral called graphite!

Who thought of putting an eraser on a pencil?

Mr. Hyman L. Lipman of Philadelphia. And he became rich because of it. Back in the 1850s pencils and erasers had already been invented. But Lipman was the first to think of fastening them together. In 1858 Lipman took out a patent on his idea. His pencils became very popular. With them people didn't have to hunt around for an eraser each time they made a mistake. The fortune Lipman made from his pencils would be worth more than one million dollars in today's money.

What makes a ball-point pen write?

The little ball in the point has something to do with it. When you write, the ball rolls around. As the ball rolls, it picks up ink from a long tube inside the pen. The ball then transfers the ink to the paper.

Before the ball-point pen could be perfected, scientists had to invent a special kind of ink to put in it. Old-fashioned writing ink was too watery. And it leaked out of ball-point pens. So scientists made the ink thicker, like syrup. Then it didn't leak.

Ball-point pens were invented as long ago as 1888. Yet people didn't use them much until the 1950s.

IN 1880 THE BOYS AT THE AGENCY WEREN'T ON THE BALL! HEE HEE HEE!

Who invented the printing press?

A German named Johannes Gutenberg (yo-HAHN-us GOOT-un-berg) around the year 1440. Before that, Europeans carved wood blocks and pressed them against paper or copied books by hand. Gutenberg's press used a separate piece of metal type for each letter. The pieces of type could be moved around to form different words. Once the type was put in order, the printer inked it. Then he placed a piece of paper over it and turned a giant-sized screw. This pressed a big wooden block against the paper. In that way the ink left its mark on the paper.

Johannes Gutenberg removes a printed page from his press.

Some modern printing presses are bigger than a bus.
And they use whole truckloads of paper and ink!

How do modern books get printed?

The greatest advances in printing have been made in the methods of preparing the type for the press. Computers, photography, and even laser beams are used today. For printing large numbers of newspapers, magazines, and books quickly, very big automatic presses are used. The printer just pushes some buttons. Then the press prints several thousand copies of a newspaper in an hour. But modern printing presses are still based on Gutenberg's idea, though they are much bigger and faster than the old-fashioned presses.

How does a typewriter work?

A typewriter has little pieces of metal in the shape of letters, numbers, and other symbols. These press an inky ribbon or tape against a piece of paper. The little pieces of metal are called type. They are attached to levers called typebars. The buttons that you tap with your fingers are called keys. The keys are connected to the typebars by rods and levers. When you push down on a key, a typebar pops up and whacks its piece of type against the inky ribbon. The type makes its mark on the paper.

Most electric typewriters work in a similar way. But the electric motor makes everything work much more quickly and easily.

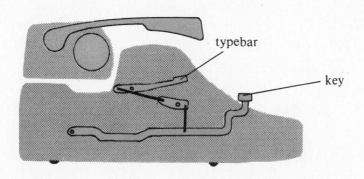

typebar

key

! You probably write about 20 words a minute.
The fastest typists can type 150 to 200 words a minute! !

How do Venetian blinds open and close?

A machine inside the Venetian blinds makes them open and close. The machine works with a pulley. A pulley is a wheel that has a groove around the rim to hold a cord or rope.

To make the blinds open or close, you pull a cord. This sets off a chain of events. The cord turns a pulley. The pulley turns a screw. The screw turns a gear. The turning gear changes the slant of the top strip, or slat. This changes the slant of all the slats in the blind. So, more or less light can come in.

rail

pulley

top slat

cord

slat

I THINK THEY MIGHT LOOK GREAT IN MY DEN.

How do Venetian blinds go up and down?

With a cord and pulleys. To make the blinds go up or down, you pull the cord down or let it go up. This cord is different from the one you pull to open or close Venetian blinds. This cord is threaded through a few pulleys in the heavy rail above the top slat. It also passes down through holes in all the slats to the bottom bar. When you pull down on the cord, it pulls the bottom bar up. And with it, up go as many of the slats as you like.

What makes a roller coaster go?

Gravity—the force that makes things fall toward the ground. Roller coasters are powered by gravity, except at the very beginning of the ride. To get started, the roller-coaster cars hook on to a chain. It pulls them to the top of the first hill. The chain can pull the cars because gears connect it to a motor on the ground. When the cars get to the top of the first hill, the hooks let go. Then the cars roll down. They go faster and faster until they reach the bottom. As the cars go up the next hill, they slow down. The same force of gravity that makes the cars go faster when they are coasting down makes them go slower when they are coasting up. Each hill that the cars go up is a little lower than the hill that the cars just rolled down. This is because gravity does not let the cars roll to a place that is as high as the hill they just came from.

What makes an elevator work?

When you step into an elevator and push the button, an electric motor starts up. The motor is in a room at the top of the building. The motor pulls a set of cables that lift the box in which you are riding. This box is called the elevator car. Each cable is a rope made of wires twisted or woven together. The cables run over pulleys attached to the motor. Then the cables go back down the shaft to a counterweight. A counterweight is a weight that balances the car. When the car goes up, the counterweight goes down. When the car goes down, the counterweight goes up. An elevator has an automatic brake that stops the car if it begins to fall.

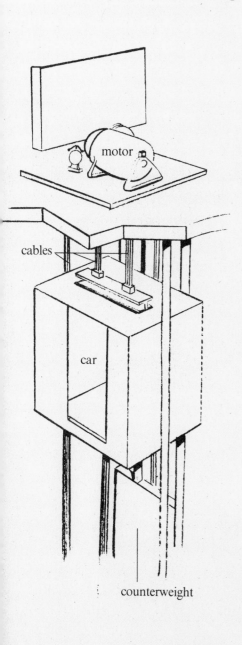

E. G. OTIS

 In 1900 the first escalator was installed by
the Otis Elevator Company at the Paris Exposition.
The machine was moved to the Gimbel Brothers' store in
Philadelphia in 1901, where it was used until 1939.

Where do the steps on an escalator go after they reach the end?

They go underneath the escalator. Then they come out again at the other end. All the steps are hooked together like the links of a chain. Underneath, where you can't see, each step has wheels that run along tracks. These tracks are very much like the tracks that trains run on. An escalator gets its power from a strong electric motor. The motor is connected to a gear that moves a chain. This chain is just like the chain that connects the pedals and rear wheel of a bicycle. But it's a lot bigger. The chain is connected to the escalator's steps. The motor turns the gear, and the gear moves the chain. The moving chain makes the steps move along the tracks.

How does a sewing machine make stitches?

A sewing machine pokes thread through pieces of cloth. Then it ties the thread in loops. In that way, the thread will stay in place and hold the cloth together. When you sew by hand, you use one thread. But when you sew with a sewing machine, you use two threads. One thread comes down from the top of the machine and goes through the eye of the needle. The other thread is in the bottom of the machine. It is wound on a small spool called a bobbin. The needle pushes the top thread down through the cloth. When the needle is down as far as it can go, a hook in the bottom of the machine catches the top thread. The hook wraps the top thread around the bottom thread, and a stitch is made. When the needle goes back up, it pulls the top thread and makes the stitch tight.

Who invented the sewing machine?

Everyone thinks of the American Elias Howe as the inventor of the sewing machine. Howe's machine (patented in 1846) was the most successful. But it was not the first. A sewing machine was patented as long ago as 1790 by Thomas Saint of England. His machine was made for sewing leather. A tool called an awl punched holes in the leather. A needle stitched through the holes.

Elias Howe

When was the zipper invented?

Whitcomb L. Judson of Chicago took out a patent on the first zipper in 1893. But the early zippers weren't very reliable. Often they would jam, so that they couldn't be opened or closed. Sometimes they would suddenly pop open all by themselves. A person would find himself standing around with his underwear showing. Other people would point and giggle. It was safer to wear clothes with buttons. But then in 1913 Gideon Sundback of Sweden invented an improved zipper that was reliable. Still, zippers didn't really become popular until the 1930s. That's when the leading fashion designers began to use them.

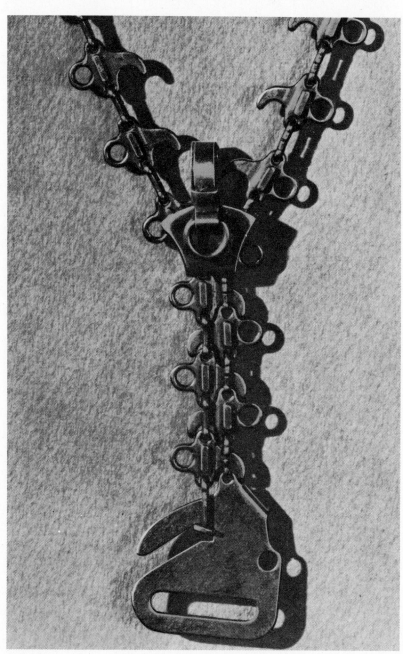

Judson zipper

How does a zipper work?

A zipper has two rows of teeth that lock together when you zip it up. A little bump on the top of each tooth fits into a little hole in the bottom of the tooth above.

The part that you pull up and down is called the slide. Inside it is a Y-shaped track. The two rows of teeth run through this track. Inside the track, the teeth bend and the spaces between them become wider. The wider spaces let the teeth fit together when you pull the slide up. They let the teeth come apart when you pull the slide down. On some zippers, the teeth are made of metal. Other zippers have plastic teeth, and each row of teeth looks like a long, thin spring.

What does a cotton gin do?

A cotton gin is a machine that takes the seeds out of cotton. After the cotton is picked, the seeds have to be taken out. Then the fluffy white fibers can be made into thread, yarn, and cloth. Before Eli Whitney invented the cotton gin in 1793, people had to take out the seeds by hand. This was very slow work. It limited the amount of cotton a farmer could grow and sell. Whitney's cotton gin used a hand crank to turn two rollers. One roller had metal claws to pull the cotton off the seeds. The other roller had bristles to brush the cotton off the claws. Then it could be gathered up. Modern cotton gins are larger and faster than Eli Whitney's. But they are based on his idea.

Cotton gin

ELI WHITNEY

Did Eli Whitney invent anything besides the cotton gin?

Yes. Eli Whitney invented a way of making things quickly. It is called mass production.

In the 1700s and before, people built machines one at a time. This process was slow. And no two machines came out exactly alike. Whitney changed all that. He started mass production of guns called muskets. He made batches of musket parts at once. He made all the barrels exactly alike. He made all the triggers exactly alike, and so on. In this way, a factory worker could take one of each part and put together a musket. Other workers could each specialize in making one kind of part. Whitney showed his idea to the United States Government in 1798. He was hired to make 10,000 muskets for the army. Modern factories still use Whitney's idea to make almost anything you can think of.

Workers using mass-produced parts on car assembly line

How did factories make their machines run before engines and motors were developed?

They used water wheels. This meant that factories had to be built close to a fast-flowing stream or river. A water wheel was made of wood. It had paddles or buckets around the rim. Part of the wheel was always in the water. As the stream flowed, water pushed against the paddles or buckets. It made the wheel turn. The wheel was attached to an axle called a drive shaft. Drive shafts were often very large. Some were made from the whole trunk of a tall tree. The drive shaft reached from the water wheel to the inside of the factory. When the water wheel turned, it made the drive shaft run the machines. In many factories, the drive shaft was used to turn other drive shafts. These other drive shafts reached upstairs and downstairs and all through the factory. In that way many machines could run at the same time.

BETTER NOT GET TOO CLOSE TO THAT WATER WHEEL, PIG-PEN!

RIGHT... IF HE EVER GOT WASHED, HIS OWN MOTHER WOULDN'T RECOGNIZE HIM.... HA HA HA...

Sound, Light, and Air

What is sound?

Sound is what you hear when something vibrates—moves back and forth quickly. If you stretch a rubber band and twang it, you can see the vibrations that cause the sound. You can also see them when you pluck a guitar string.

Anything that vibrates makes the air around it vibrate. The vibrating air makes the insides of your ears vibrate. That's how you hear. Usually you can't see any vibrations when you hear a sound. But the vibrations are still there. Sound vibrations travel through most other materials, as well as through air.

Why are some sounds low and others high?

The sound coming from a vibrating object will be high or low depending on how many vibrations it makes each second. A low sound, like that made by a foghorn, has slow vibrations. A high sound, like that made by a whistle, has fast vibrations. The lowest sounds that most people can hear have about 20 vibrations per (each) second. The highest sounds people can hear have about 20,000 vibrations per second. Some animals, such as bats and dolphins, can hear very high sounds—more than 100,000 vibrations per second. The scientific word for the number of vibrations per second is "hertz." It is abbreviated Hz. A scientist would say people can hear sounds between 20 and 20,000 hertz.

How do musical instruments make sounds?

All musical instruments make air vibrate. But they don't all do it in the same way. Some have strings that vibrate. Others have small pieces of wood called reeds that vibrate. With some instruments, the vibrations come from the player's lips. Drums, cymbals, and xylophones vibrate when somebody strikes them.

Most instruments are made so that the player can control how high or low the sound will be.

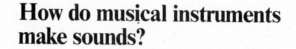

LOW SOUNDS...
HIGH SOUNDS...
GOOD GRIEF, IT'S
SOUND POLLUTION!

How does a piano work?

Attached to every piano key is a hammer. This is a piece of wood covered with a felt pad. When you press a key, the hammer hits a small group of metal strings. Most pianos have 230 strings.

The pitch (highness or lowness of the sound) of each string depends on how long and thick the string is and how tightly it is stretched. Short, thin strings have a higher pitch than long, thick strings. The tighter you stretch a string, the higher its pitch will be. Some of the strings are wrapped with wire to make them vibrate more slowly.

In 1935, a giant-sized piano was built.
Its longest string was 9 feet 11 inches (about 3 meters).
That's probably more than twice your height!

How does a guitar make music?

A guitar has strings that make sounds when you pluck them with your fingers. The strings are stretched across a pear-shaped box. Without this box, the strings would make a very faint sound. With the box, the sound is amplified (AMP-luh-fied), made louder.

The pitch of a guitar note depends on two things: the thickness and the tightness of the strings. In that way a guitar is like a piano. But on a guitar, you can change the pitch by pressing a string with your finger. When you do this, you are cutting short the part of the string that vibrates. So, in a way, you are making the string shorter. Banjos, mandolins, and ukuleles work in much the same way.

Violin

Does a violin work the same way as a guitar?

Not quite. A violin has strings like a guitar. When you play a violin, you control the pitch by pressing on the strings—as you do with a guitar. But instead of plucking the strings to make them vibrate, you rub a bow across the strings. The bow is a wooden stick with horsehairs stretched between the ends. Sound vibrations are made when the hairs rub on the violin strings.

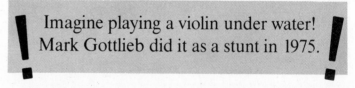

Imagine playing a violin under water! Mark Gottlieb did it as a stunt in 1975.

What is a wind instrument?

A wind instrument is any instrument that makes a sound when someone blows into it. A horn, a kazoo, and a saxophone are all wind instruments.

A wind instrument has a body made of a long or short tube. When you blow into the instrument, air vibrates inside the tube. The longer the tube, the lower the pitch. Most wind instruments have push buttons on, or holes in, the tube. That's where you put your fingers when you play the instrument. When you press a button or uncover a hole, the pitch is changed. The pitch changes because the amount of space left for the air to vibrate in changes.

There are two main kinds of wind instruments. They are called brass instruments and woodwind instruments.

53

What are brass instruments like?

Bugles, trumpets, cornets, trombones, tubas, French horns, and sousaphones are brass instruments. They all have very long tubes that are folded back and forth or curled around and around. This makes the instrument easier to carry than if the long tube were straight. As you might guess, brass instruments are made of brass.

If you want to play a brass instrument, you must press your lips together and make a buzzing sound like "p-f-f-f-t" when you blow into the tube. When you go "p-f-f-f-t," your lips vibrate. This makes the air in the instrument vibrate.

Hunting horn

L.V. BEETHOVEN

TROMBONE

FRENCH HORN

TUBA

THIS IS A GREAT WAY TO MEET SOME REALLY NEAT CHICKS.

How are woodwind instruments played?

Woodwind players don't go "p-f-f-f-t." Instead, they blow air across one or two thin pieces of wood called reeds. Or else they blow across a hole at one end of the instrument. Clarinets, oboes, bassoons, and saxophones are played by blowing across reeds. Blowing makes the reeds vibrate. Flutes and piccolos are played by blowing across a hole. Blowing across the hole makes the air inside the instrument vibrate.

Once all woodwinds were made of wood. Today, some are made of plastic or metal.

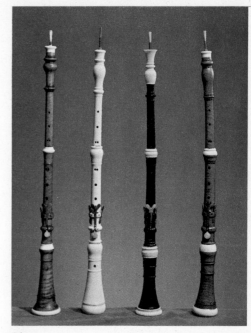

Oboes

55

How does a stethoscope help a doctor listen to your heart?

A stethoscope lets the doctor listen with both ears. Before stethoscopes were invented, doctors had to listen to hearts by pressing one ear against the patient's chest. Now they can use both ears and hear better.

A stethoscope has two listening pieces to help the doctor hear different kinds of sounds. The small disc piece is good for listening to very low-pitched sounds. The large disc piece is good for listening to higher sounds. The sounds travel from the listening pieces through rubber tubes to the doctor's ears. The next time you go for a checkup, ask the doctor to let you listen to your heart with the stethoscope.

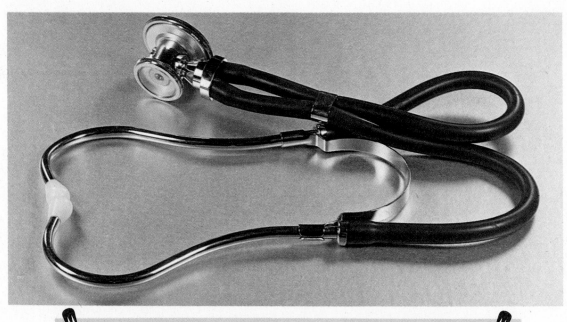

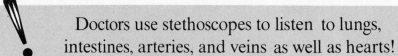

Doctors use stethoscopes to listen to lungs, intestines, arteries, and veins as well as hearts!

What is a prism?

A prism is a bar of glass with flat sides. A good prism has no bubbles or ripples in it. When a beam of sunlight passes through a prism, the light spreads out into separate beams of color. The colors are the same as you would see in a rainbow—red, orange, yellow, green, blue, and violet. In fact, a rainbow in the sky is caused by drops of water in the air that act like prisms. A drop of water can change sunlight into colored beams of light, just like a prism.

How does a prism cause a rainbow?

A beam of sunlight is really a mixture of light waves of many colors. Light travels in the form of waves. Each color of light has its own kind of wave. Red light waves are long. Violet light waves are short. The other colors are in between.

When light waves enter a prism, they bend. And they bend again when they come out of the other side of the prism. The various colors bend by different amounts. Because of this, the colors spread out as they pass through the prism. The colors line up side by side instead of being mixed together. And you can see the separate colors of the rainbow.

Light shining through prism

57

Why does a mirror show a picture of what's in front of it?

A mirror shows a picture, called a reflected image, because the mirror has a thick shiny silver-colored coating behind the glass. The silver-colored coating does two things:

1. It keeps light waves from passing through the mirror. Since they can't go through, they bounce back toward your eyes.

2. It makes the mirror *very* shiny.

When light waves bounce off a dull, unshiny surface, they scatter and go every which way. But when the waves bounce off something shiny, they don't scatter.

When you stand in front of a mirror, light waves move from you to the shiny mirror. The light waves then bounce right back off the mirror in exactly the same way they hit the mirror. And you see yourself!

58

How does a magnifying glass make things look big?

A magnifying glass plays a trick on your eyes. It does this by changing the direction of light waves coming from the object you are looking at. The curved surfaces of the glass bend the waves, and it appears to your eyes that the waves are coming from a big object.

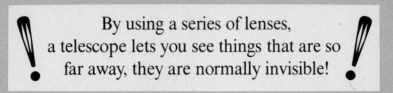

! ! By using a series of lenses, a telescope lets you see things that are so far away, they are normally invisible! ! !

! ! By using two or three magnifying lenses, a microscope lets you see things that are so small, they are normally invisible! ! !

How do eyeglasses and contact lenses help some people see better?

When you look at something, you see it because waves of light are coming from it. When some of these enter your eye, they form a picture of what you are looking at. This picture appears on the back surface of the inside eye.

When light waves enter the eye, they pass through the curved front end called the cornea. Then they pass through a part called the lens. The combination of cornea and lens is supposed to focus, or aim, the light waves so that the picture on the back of the eye will be clear and sharp. Some people's eyes cannot do this very well. So they have blurry vision. Other people have eyeballs that are either too long or too short from front to back. If an eyeball is too long or too short, it is hard for it to form a good picture on the back surface of the eye.

Eyeglasses and contact lenses are extra glass or plastic lenses put in front of the eyes' own lenses. The glasses or contacts help eyes with blurry vision by doing part of the work of aiming or bending the light waves. Then the waves can come together at the right place at the back of the eye.

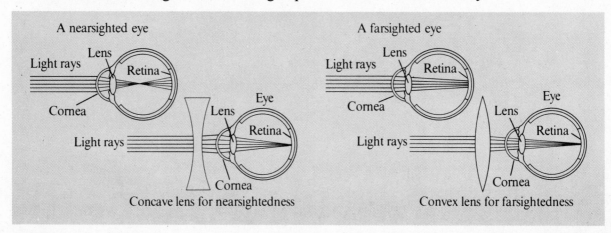

How are bifocals different from other eyeglasses?

Regular eyeglasses have one simple lens for each eye. The lens helps a person see either nearby things better or faraway things better. Bifocals have one lens with two parts for each eye. One part helps someone see nearby things better. Another part helps the person see faraway things better.

Benjamin Franklin invented bifocals in 1785. Before that time, people who needed glasses to see clearly both far and near things had to carry around two pairs. But with bifocals such people need only one pair.

Benjamin Franklin

How does a camera make photographs?

A camera works very much like an eye. Light waves enter the front of a camera through a set of lenses. The lenses focus the light to form a picture on the inside back wall of the camera. To make photographs, you need a roll of film in your camera. Photographic film is a strip of plastic coated with special chemicals. These chemicals change when light hits them. The camera is made to hold part of the roll of film against the back wall of the camera. When you press the button to take a picture, light comes into the camera for a very short time—usually less than a second. The light waves shine on the film. They change the chemicals so that a picture will appear when the film is developed.

How is film developed?

When you take your film to be developed, the person you give it to sends it to a laboratory. There the film is taken into a darkroom and unrolled. The developing has to be done in the dark because light would ruin your pictures. The film is dunked into a tank of liquid chemicals. These chemicals change the color of the chemicals on your film in such a way that pictures are formed. These pictures are called negatives. Negatives show the objects in the picture with their right shapes but the wrong colors.

Next, each negative is placed over a piece of photographic paper. Photographic paper is coated with chemicals on one side. This is the paper from which your finished photographs will be made. When the negative is over the paper, a light is turned on for a few seconds. The light shines through the negative and casts a picture on the photographic paper. The picture is like a shadow of the negative. The paper remains blank, but the light shining on it causes invisible changes in the chemicals.

Next, the paper is placed in a pan of liquid chemicals. These liquids change the chemicals on the paper. Slowly, as the chemicals change, the finished photograph appears.

63

X-RAY TUBE   CATHODE PLATE   ROTATING DISC TARGET

GLASS BULB   ANODE   OIL FILLING WINDOW

How can x-rays take a picture of a person's insides?

X-rays are like light waves, but they are much shorter. Scientists have built machines that shoot beams of x-rays just as flashlights shoot beams of visible light. Machines that shoot beams of x-rays are called x-ray machines. When light waves hit a person, they bounce off. But when x-rays hit a person, they go right through—just like light through a piece of glass. In this way, light waves and x-rays behave differently. But when light waves or x-rays hit a piece of photographic film, they behave the same. Both kinds of waves change the chemicals on the film. To make an x-ray picture of a person's insides, the x-ray machine shoots rays through the person onto a piece of photographic film. When the film is developed, it shows a shadowy picture of all the bones and other things inside the body.

The man who discovered x-rays, Wilhelm Roentgen (RENT-gun), didn't understand what they were. That's why he called the rays *x*!

I WONDER IF THAT MEANT THEY WERE X-RATED! HEE HEE HEE...

64

Series of photographs taken of running horse

What makes movies move?

If you look at a piece of movie film, you can see that it is just a long strip of photographs on a plastic strip. Each photograph is a tiny bit different from those on each side of it. If the film is of someone running or jumping or diving, you can see that the arms and legs are in different positions in different pictures. When you show the film in a projector, the projector flashes the pictures on a screen one at a time. The pictures flash on the screen very fast. You see 16 or more separate photos in just one second. When the pictures flash by that fast, your brain can't tell that your eyes are looking at many separate photos. You think you are looking at only one picture—a picture that moves.

65

How are cartoon movies made?

Cartoon characters are just drawings, and they can't move. But it is possible to play a trick on people's eyes so that it looks as if the characters are moving. To do this, artists draw thousands of pictures on separate clear plastic sheets called cels. Each picture shows a character in a slightly different position.

For each scene, the artists paint a background. One or more cels are put on top of the background. The combination is photographed by a special movie camera. (It takes only one picture each time a button is pressed. The usual movie camera keeps taking one picture after another.) Then the cels just photographed are taken off the background. Cels that look just a bit different from the first are placed over the same background. A second picture is photographed. In fact, one picture is taken for each tiny bit of movement a character is supposed to be making. When the film is shown through a movie projector, the characters appear to move. If you look at a strip of cartoon film, you can see how the characters change slightly from one picture to the next.

Who invented movies?

No one knows for sure. In the 1880s and 1890s many people were working on ways to make and project moving pictures. In 1891 Thomas Edison, the man who invented the electric light, built the first kinetoscope (kin-ET-uh-scope). This was a cabinet with a peephole. Inside were reels of film that turned. One person at a time looked into the peephole to see the movie. Some people believe that Edison's helper, William Dickson, invented the kinetoscope—not Edison.

What is a laser?

A laser is a machine that shoots a thin, very high-powered beam of light. This beam is called a laser beam. Some laser beams are so powerful that they can burn holes in metal.

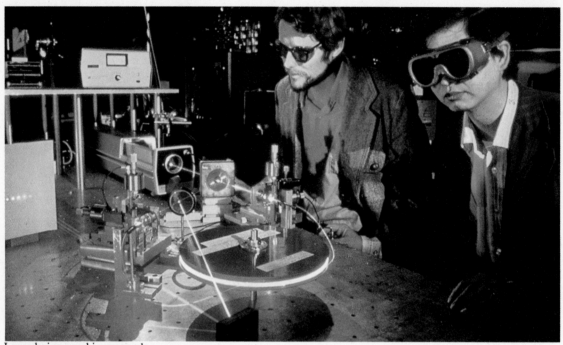

Laser being used in research

How does a laser work?

A laser beam starts out as a flash of ordinary light from a bright lamp. Light is a kind of energy, and it travels in waves or ripples. Ordinary light waves are jumbled. They spread out and go in all directions. A laser unjumbles the waves. It packs them side by side so that they all ripple up and down together. When the light waves are packed together like this, they will travel in a very straight line and not spread out. These light waves make up a laser beam.

How do people use lasers?

Many uses have been found for lasers. Laser beams are much hotter than other light beams. Their heat can be used to weld or cut tiny things. Sometimes surgeons use a laser instead of a knife to perform delicate operations on the insides of people's eyes.

Laser beams can travel farther than other light beams. In one test, a laser was used to shoot down an aircraft two miles away. Scientists can measure exactly how far it is from the earth to the moon by bouncing a laser beam off the moon.

How does a thermometer tell the temperature?

The most common type of thermometer is a hollow glass tube that holds a liquid. Usually the liquid is mercury or colored alcohol. When the temperature goes up, the liquid expands, or gets bigger. It takes up more space inside the tube. So the liquid rises in the tube. When the temperature falls, the liquid contracts, or gets smaller. It fills less space. So the liquid moves down the tube.

Along the glass tube are numbers. These numbers mark off small sections called degrees. The symbol for degree is a tiny circle next to the number, like this: 32°.

Sometimes you will see 50° F. or 10° C. The F. stands for Fahrenheit (FAIR-un-hite). The C. stands for Celsius (SELL-see-us). These are the most common kinds of thermometer measurements. Each kind uses a different range of numbers. But they both measure the same thing—how hot or cold it is where the thermometer is.

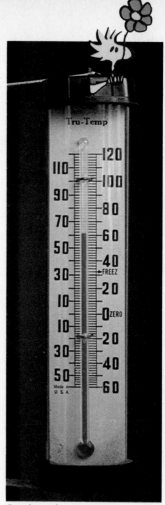

Outdoor thermometer

A man named Gustave Brickner went for a swim in a river every day, no matter what the temperature. On January 24, 1963, he swam when the air temperature was 18° below zero Fahrenheit (−28° C.)!

69

Do all thermometers look alike?

No. For example, oven and refrigerator thermometers are called bimetallic (by-muh-TAL-ick) thermometers. "Bimetallic" means two metals. This kind of thermometer has a spring made of two metals.

Metals expand when heated and contract when cooled. A bimetallic thermometer uses two different kinds of metal. One expands and contracts more than the other. Thin strips of the two metals are joined side by side. Then they are rolled up to make the spring. The spring is connected to a pointer. When the temperature rises, one of the metal strips winds up tighter than the other. This causes the pointer to move in one direction and not the other. The pointer swings to a higher number. When the temperature falls, the pointer moves in the other direction. It points to a lower number.

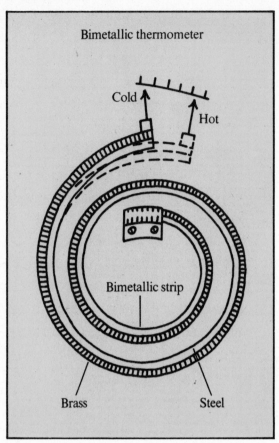

Bimetallic thermometer

Cold

Hot

Bimetallic strip

Brass

Steel

How does a furnace make a whole house warm?

When coal, gas, or oil is burned inside a furnace, heat is produced. The heat can be moved from the furnace to other places in a house in at least three different ways.

1. The furnace heats air. A blower pushes warm air from the furnace through tunnels called ducts. The ducts lead to openings in all parts of the house.

2. The furnace heats water in a boiler. When the water boils, it turns to steam. The pressure of the steam makes it go through pipes to radiators in each room.

3. The furnace heats water in a boiler. A pump then sends the hot water through pipes to radiators. When the radiators become hot, they warm the air in the rooms.

How does a radiator warm a room?

A hot radiator warms the air next to it. The warmer the air gets, the lighter it becomes. Light air rises. So the warm, light air rises toward the ceiling. That should leave airless space near the floor by the radiator. But the gap is instantly filled by cool air that moves in from other parts of the room. This cool air becomes warm next to the radiator. And then *it* rises. The rising of the warm air and the movement of cool air toward the radiator is called convection (kun-VECK-shun). Convection is like a tiny wind that spreads the heat of the radiator all through the air in the room.

Red pieces of paper in boiling water show convection pattern

WHEW, SUDDENLY I'M VERY WARM. I WONDER IF I HAVE A FEVER.

GET OFF THAT HOT RADIATOR, STUPID. YOU'RE BLOCKING ALL THE HEAT.

71

What is solar heating?

Solar heating uses wave energy that comes to us from the sun. In recent years, oil and gas have become scarce and expensive. People have realized that the burning of coal pollutes the air. So scientists and inventors have been searching for new ways to heat houses. One way is to capture heat from sunshine. Even in winter, there is a lot of heat coming to us in the form of waves from the sun. The problem is how to catch this heat energy and bring it indoors before it gets away.

How can people catch the sun's heat?

The most common solar heat collector is a low, flat box. It has a glass or plastic window on top. Most of the sun's light waves can pass easily through the glass or plastic. The inside of the box is painted black. This is because dark colors absorb, or soak up, the incoming light waves. Light colors reflect the waves, or make them bounce away.

The collector box is placed outdoors, usually on a roof facing the sun. The box is sealed very tightly. So none of the heat that enters through the window can get away. When the sun is shining, the box becomes hot inside. This is true even in winter.

The next step is to bring the heat from the box into the house. This is done with water pipes and a pump. Cool water is pumped from the house to pipes inside the collector box. The heat in the collector warms the water in the pipes. A pipe takes the warm water back into the house. There it can be pumped through a radiator, or used for washing or bathing. Sometimes it goes into a storage tank. If the water stayed too long in the tank, it would get cold. So it is pumped back up to the collector box to get heated again.

What makes a furnace turn on and off by itself?

Furnaces in houses and other buildings are controlled by thermostats (THUR-muh-stats). A thermostat turns the furnace on when the building is cool and off when the building is warm. A thermostat has a bimetallic spring, just like the thermometer you use in an oven or refrigerator. When the room temperature rises, the spring stretches in one direction. It turns off an electric switch. When the temperature falls, the spring stretches in the other direction. It turns the switch back on. You can set a thermostat to keep a house at any fairly steady temperature that you choose.

What other things use thermostats?

Many things that work by heating or cooling use thermostats. Refrigerators, air conditioners, ovens, electric frying pans, and electric blankets all have thermostats. If you set an air conditioner's thermostat at 75° F. (24° C.), it will keep the temperature of the room fairly steady. As soon as the air gets cooler, the air conditioner shuts off. As soon as the air gets warmer, the air conditioner turns on again.

What makes a refrigerator cold inside?

A refrigerator is a machine for taking heat out of a closed box. Cold is what is left in the box after the heat is taken out. The working of a refrigerator is based on one special fact: a liquid absorbs, or soaks up, heat when it evaporates (ih-VAP-uh-rates). When a liquid evaporates, it changes into a gas.

A refrigerator has a metal tube filled with a liquid that evaporates very fast. Part of the tube is inside the food box. Part of the tube is outside—underneath the refrigerator or on the back. If the inside of the food box gets warm, a thermostat turns on the refrigerator's motor. This makes the liquid flow through the tube. When the liquid enters the part of the tube that is *in* the food box, the liquid evaporates. It soaks up heat. Because the liquid has evaporated, the tube leading out of the food box is filled with gas. The tube leads to a compressor (come-PRESS-ur). A compressor squeezes the gas and changes it back into a liquid. When the gas is changed into a liquid, it gives off heat. So the compressor becomes hot. The heat goes into the air of the kitchen as the liquid moves through the part of the tube outside the refrigerator. The liquid again enters the food box. There it evaporates and soaks up more heat

How does an air conditioner make a room cool?

An air conditioner works exactly the same as a refrigerator. But instead of taking heat out of a food box and putting it into the kitchen, it takes heat out of a room and puts it outdoors.

Part of a room-sized air conditioner is inside a window. This part has a cold tube filled with evaporating liquid. Part of the air conditioner is outside the window. This part has a compressor and a tube that gives off heat. An air conditioner also has a fan that blows air past the cold tube and out into the room. In this way all the air in the room gets a chance to be cooled by being blown past the cold tube.

How does a Thermos bottle keep milk cold?

"Thermos" is a brand name for a vacuum (VACK-yoom) bottle. A vacuum bottle works by insulating (IN-suh-late-ing) whatever you store in it. This means that when you store something cold, like milk, the bottle lets in very little heat. When you store something hot, like cocoa, the bottle lets very little heat get out.

A vacuum bottle is built like a bottle within a bottle. There is a narrow space between the two bottles. Almost all the air has been pumped out of this space. An empty space with no air or almost no air in it is called a vacuum. The vacuum keeps air from touching the inside bottle. It is important to keep the amount of air small because air can carry heat to cold things and take heat away from hot things.

Some heat can get through a vacuum. But much of this heat is blocked by the bottle's shiny, silvery coating. Heat, which travels in waves, bounces off shiny, silvery things. The bottle, being made of glass, also helps to insulate what is in it. Heat does not travel easily through glass.

How does a percolator make coffee?

A percolator is a machine for automatically pouring hot water on ground-up coffee beans. When hot water washes over the ground coffee, part of the beans dissolve in the water. That becomes the liquid coffee that people drink.

When the water in the bottom of a percolator starts to boil, it gives off bubbles of steam. Steam bubbles are lighter than water, and so they float up from the bottom. Most of them go up through the hollow tube that holds up the coffee basket. The bubbles rush up the narrow stem. Any water that gets in the way is pushed up the stem, too. That water squirts out the top of the stem. Then it drips down through the coffee basket. As it passes over the ground coffee, it becomes coffee-flavored.

79

How does a washing machine get clothes clean?

All a washer really does is make dirty clothes flop around in soapy water for a few minutes. It is the soap that gets the clothes clean. The most important part of a top-loader is called the agitator (AJ-ih-tay-tur). The agitator sticks up in the middle of the tub. It turns one way and then the other, back and forth. The paddles on the agitator poke and stir the clothes so that they move around in the water. After several minutes, the dirty water is pumped out. Clean water comes in to rinse the soap out of the clothes. Then the rinse water is pumped out, and the clothes are ready for drying.

IT'S WASHDAY!

HOW LONG WILL IT TAKE? I'LL NEVER MAKE IT! AAUGH!...

ZIP!

How does a drier take the water out of wet laundry?

Wet clothes become dry because the water that is in them evaporates. When water evaporates, it changes to water vapor, a kind of gas, and goes off into the air. A clothes drier is a machine that makes evaporation take place quickly. It does this by blowing air on the clothes while they are tumbling around. Usually the air is warmed by a gas flame or an electric heater. This makes the water in the clothes evaporate quickly. Heat makes the tiny particles of water jump off into the air. Also, hot air can hold more water vapor than cold air can.

WHEW!... SAVED THROUGH THE MIRACLE OF MODERN LAUNDERING!

What makes a fire hose squirt far?

Two things—a pump and a nozzle. The pump is inside the fire truck that carries the hose. The pump pushes the water through the hose. The water goes through the hose in a wide, heavy, slow stream. But then the water comes to the metal nozzle at the end of the hose. The nozzle is much narrower than the hose. The nozzle squeezes the moving water into a thin, fast stream. Such a stream can go farther than a thick, slow stream. If you have a garden hose, try using it with a nozzle and without a nozzle. You will see that the nozzle makes the water squirt farther.

How does a water pistol shoot?

The trigger of a water pistol is connected to a small pump. When you pull the trigger, the pump makes some water move through a tube. Then the water squirts out through a nozzle in the front of the pistol. When you let go of the trigger, a spring pushes the trigger out and also refills the pump. You are then ready for the next shot.

How does a scuba-diving tank work?

The scuba tank holds compressed air. "Compressed" means that a lot is squeezed into a small space. If you let all the air out of a scuba tank, it could fill a whole room. A little bit of air at a time goes from the tank through a hose to a diver's mouth.

The most important parts of a scuba outfit are the valves. They control the amount of gas or liquid that goes through a pipe or hose. Some valves are like faucets. They start or stop the flow of liquid or gas when you turn them with your hand. A special kind of valve in a scuba outfit automatically lets the diver get more air when he goes down deep. Another special valve lets the diver breathe used air out into the water. It also doesn't let any water come in when the diver breathes in.

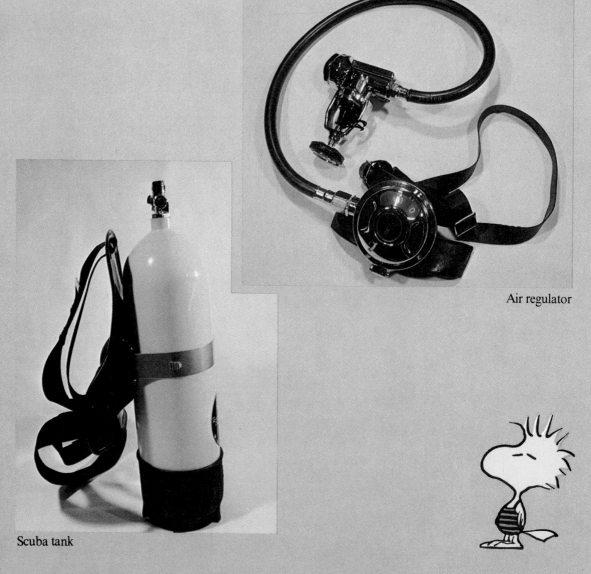

Air regulator

Scuba tank

Who invented modern scuba equipment?

Jacques Cousteau (ZHOCK koo-STOE), the famous ocean scientist who makes nature films for television. But he didn't do it all by himself. He had a partner named Emile Gagnan (ay-MEAL gah-NYOH). The two men were a perfect team. Cousteau was an ocean diver in the French navy. Gagnan was an engineer who knew a lot about all kinds of valves.

Cousteau knew that old-fashioned diving equipment was unsafe. Divers sometimes couldn't get enough air when they went down very deep. He figured that a new kind of valve was needed to control the amount of air coming out of the diver's tank. Gagnan was able to make the kind of valve Cousteau wanted. Cousteau and Gagnan completed their invention in 1943.

Jacques Cousteau (center)

What does "scuba" mean?

"Scuba" is a word made from the initials of the words "*s*elf-*c*ontained *u*nderwater *b*reathing *a*pparatus." Words made from the initials of other words are called acronyms (ACK-ruh-nimz). Acronyms help people save time in talking and writing by changing a bunch of big words into one little word.

How did the vacuum cleaner get its name?

When a vacuum cleaner is turned on, a fan keeps blowing out most of the air from its tank. A space with no air inside it is called a vacuum. A space with only a little bit of air inside it is called a partial (PAR-shul) vacuum. As the air goes out of a vacuum cleaner's tank, a partial vacuum is left. That is why the machine is called a "vacuum" cleaner.

How does a vacuum cleaner pick up dirt?

By using suction. The vacuum cleaner's fan blows air out of its tank or bag and leaves a partial vacuum inside. If you make an opening in the side of the container of a vacuum or a partial vacuum, air will rush in to fill the empty space. This is called suction.

Along with the air that rushes into a vacuum cleaner come dust and dirt. The air is blown out again. But the dust and dirt are caught in the dust bag, which is made of filter paper or finely woven cloth. When the bag is full, you can throw it away or empty it and use it again.

How can a weather forecaster tell when it is going to rain?

Weather depends on what the air is like. Weather forecasters know that clear, dry air is heavier than wet, stormy air.

Forecasters use a machine called a barometer (buh-ROM-ih-tur) to measure just how heavy the air is in any one area. There are many weather stations all over the country. In each one is a barometer. A forecaster looks at the barometer a few times each day. He or she checks to see whether the air is getting lighter or heavier. If the air is getting lighter in a certain place, that's a sign that rain is coming. If the air in a rainy place starts getting heavier, that's a sign that clear weather is coming.

How does a barometer tell how heavy the air is?

A barometer works by measuring how hard the air pushes something movable. One very popular type of barometer uses a heavy silvery liquid called mercury as the movable thing. The mercury moves up and down inside a long glass tube. Nothing else is inside this tube, not even air. The tube is sealed at the top and open at the bottom. The bottom is set in a little cup filled with mercury.

A mercury barometer works like a soda straw. When you suck on the straw, you take air out of it. But the air all around the soda presses on it. This air pressure forces the soda up inside the empty straw and into your mouth. The mercury inside the barometer tube is held up by the pressure of the outside air on the mercury in the cup. Heavy air pushes harder than light air and makes the mercury go farther up the tube. There is a yardstick alongside the tube so a person can see exactly how high the mercury stands.

Clear, heavy air will push the mercury a little more than 30 inches (76 centimeters) up the tube. Light, stormy air will push the mercury about 29 inches (about 74 centimeters) up the tube. That's not much of a difference. But it's enough to help the weather forecaster decide whether a day will be sunny or stormy.

NO, MEN. BREAKING THE GLASS IN THE BAROMETER WILL NOT STOP THE STORM...

Do all barometers have liquid in them?

No. There is a very popular type called the aneroid (AN-uh-royd) barometer. "Aneroid" means no liquid. Many people have this type of barometer in their homes, hanging on a wall or sitting on a shelf. An aneroid barometer looks something like a clock, but it has only one hand. Its numbers show how high the mercury would be if you had a mercury barometer.

The main part of an aneroid barometer is a hollow box or can. Inside is a vacuum. The sides of the box or can are made of springy metal. Air from outside the box always presses on the sides of the box. When the air presses, the sides move in. Clear, heavy air presses them in farther than stormy, light air. Levers connect the box to the hand on the front of the barometer. In this way, the hand points to a high number when the air pressure is high. It points to a low number when the air pressure is low.

Who invented the barometer?

Evangelista Torricelli (tore-ih-CHELL-lee) invented the barometer in 1643. But the first *weather-forecasting* barometer was made by Otto von Guericke (GAY-rih-keh) in the 1670s. It was about 34 feet (more than 10 meters) tall and used water instead of mercury. A water barometer needs to be much taller than a mercury barometer. That is because water weighs much less than mercury. Since water is lighter, the weight of the air pushes water higher than it pushes mercury.

Otto von Guericke

A scientist named Blaise Pascal (BLEZ pas-KALL) once made a barometer filled with red wine. He used red wine instead of water because it was easier to see inside a glass tube. Since wine weighs less than water, Pascal needed a tube 46 feet (14 meters) tall.

87

What makes a spray can squirt?

Inside a spray can is compressed gas. Compressed gas is like the air in a blown-up balloon. If you let go of the opening of the balloon, the air will rush out. The compressed gas in a spray can would also rush out. But it can't do this until you push the button on top of the can. Pressing the button is like opening a faucet. You are giving the compressed gas a place to go. As it rushes out, it pushes the liquid (paint, shaving cream, or insect killer) out before it. The liquid comes out as a fine spray. A spring makes the button pop up when you stop pressing it.

What makes a fire extinguisher squirt?

Fire extinguishers use compressed gas to make them squirt. The gas for most extinguishers is pumped in at the factory. But one type of extinguisher makes compressed gas when you turn it upside down. This type is called a soda-acid extinguisher.

The soda in soda-acid is not the kind you drink. It is a chemical called baking soda. The acid is a chemical called sulfuric (sull-FYOOR-ick) acid.

The extinguisher is filled with water. Soda is dissolved in the water. In the top of the extinguisher is a small bottle of sulfuric acid. When you turn the extinguisher upside down, the acid mixes with the water and baking soda. As a result, a lot of carbon dioxide gas is formed. It is under pressure inside the extinguisher. As soon as a compressed gas is given room, it will spread out. Because there is an opening in the extinguisher, the compressed carbon dioxide rushes out. The opening leads to a hose. The gas goes out through the hose and pushes the water out.

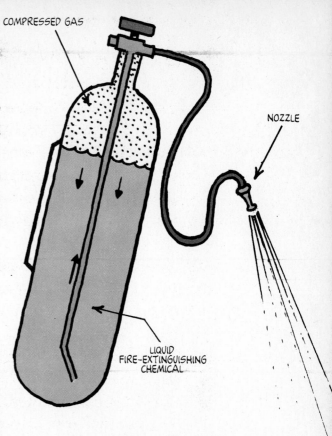

COMPRESSED GAS

NOZZLE

LIQUID FIRE-EXTINGUISHING CHEMICAL

GOOD GRIEF! IT'S ONLY PIG-PEN! I THOUGHT IT WAS A WALKING BRUSH FIRE!

How does a fire extinguisher put out fires?

Fires need two things to keep going: a gas called oxygen, and fuel. Fuel is anything that can get hot enough to burn. Some extinguishers cool the fuel. Others keep oxygen (which is in the air) away from the fuel.

Extinguishers that squirt water work mostly by cooling the fuel until it is too cold to burn. Extinguishers that squirt carbon dioxide make the fuel very cold—colder than ice. They also drive oxygen away from the fire. Some extinguishers squirt a dry chemical powder. It forms a crust on the fuel. The crust keeps oxygen away from the fuel. Another type of extinguisher coats the fuel with foam. The foam looks something like shaving cream. The foam keeps oxygen away from the fuel.

Did people have fire extinguishers 100 years ago?

Yes. People had them more than **150** years ago.

The fire extinguisher was invented by an Englishman named George Manby in 1813. His was a metal tank with water and compressed air in it. The compressed air made the water squirt out when a faucet was turned.

What machine is used to chop holes in pavement?

Have you ever heard of a jackhammer, an air hammer, or a pneumatic (new-MAT-ick) drill? Those are three names for the same machine. It is used to chop holes in sidewalks.

A jackhammer runs on compressed air. The air is pumped into the jackhammer through a hose. A trigger in the handle starts and stops the flow of air.

Inside the jackhammer is a hollow tube called a cylinder (SILL-in-dur). It looks something like a tin can. Inside the cylinder is a piece of metal called a piston. The piston can slide up and down inside the cylinder.

When the jackhammer is turned on air comes into the top of the cylinder. It pushes the piston down very hard. The piston then slams into a chisel that sticks out of the bottom of the jackhammer. The chisel is a metal bar. It is pointed on the end that touches the pavement. The hard blow of the piston drives the chisel into the pavement.

Next, air comes into the *bottom* of the cylinder and pushes the piston back up. When the piston reaches the top of the cylinder, the air changes direction again. The piston goes down and slams into the chisel again. The piston goes up and down more than 1,000 times a minute. It strikes the chisel very hard each time. Every time the piston hits the chisel, the chisel chops away a little piece of pavement.

GOOD GRIEF! IF ONLY IT DIDN'T REMIND ME OF MY DENTIST...

How does a bicycle pump work?

A bicycle pump compresses air. One common kind is made up of a handle, a cylinder, a valve, a hose, and a metal disk with a gasket around it.

A gasket is a ring that fills an open space to make a pump or pipe leakproof. A gasket is sometimes made of rubber and sometimes of metal.

When you pull up on the handle of a bicycle pump, two things happen. First, the gasket hangs down loose and limp. This lets air go past it into the lower part of the cylinder. Second, the valve closes. So the air stays squeezed inside the bottom of the cylinder.

When you push down on the handle, the gasket presses tightly against the cylinder. It makes a tight seal. The air cannot get back up past the disk. But compressed air wants to spread out. Where can it go? When you push down on the handle, the valve opens. The air rushes out through the valve into the hose. From the hose the air goes into your bicycle tire.

What makes a popgun shoot?

Popguns work on compressed air. When you pull the trigger, a spring pushes a piston forward inside the barrel. All the air in the gun barrel is squeezed into a tiny space. This makes a lot of pressure build up. The pressure is so great that the cork at the end of the barrel can't hold the air in. The cork shoots out, and you hear a loud popping sound at the same time. The popping sound is really a small explosion. An explosion is what happens when a compressed gas suddenly bursts out of the place where it was held.

How does a car's brake pedal stop the car?

When a driver steps on a brake pedal, a chain of events begins. The pedal pushes a lever. The lever pushes a piston in a cylinder full of liquid. The piston pushes the liquid into four hoses. Each hose leads to one of the four wheels of the car. The liquid flows into a cylinder next to each wheel. There the liquid pushes more pistons. These pistons push curved pieces of metal against cylinders called brake drums. The brake drums are attached to the wheels. The rubbing of the metal slows down the turning of the wheels. So the car slows down and finally stops. When the driver stops pushing the brake pedal, springs pull the curved pieces of metal away from the brake drums. Then the wheels are free to turn again.

Do trains have the same kind of brakes as cars?

Not exactly. Trains need very powerful brakes—much more powerful than the pressure of one person pushing on a pedal with one foot. Train brakes use compressed air. The compressor is in the front of the train's locomotive. Hoses take the air to all the wheels. When the driver puts on the brakes, compressed air rushes into the hoses. The air pushes against some pistons. These pistons push curved pieces of metal against the wheels to slow down their turning.

Big trucks use the same kind of brakes as trains.

What makes a car-lifting machine go up and down?

You have probably seen the machine used in gasoline stations to lift a car into the air. It has a big, shiny metal tube that comes up out of the floor. That metal tube is really a giant piston. The piston fits into a pipe or cylinder buried in the floor. When the mechanic wants to lift the car, he turns on a pump. This pump forces liquid into the cylinder and pushes the piston up. When the car is raised high enough, the mechanic closes a kind of faucet called a valve. This keeps the liquid in the cylinder. The liquid keeps the piston from sliding back down into the floor. Then the mechanic turns off the pump. Now it is safe for him to go under the car and fix it. The car can't fall as long as liquid stays in the cylinder. When the mechanic wants to let the car down, he opens the valve. The liquid slowly leaves the cylinder and goes into a storage tank. As the liquid leaves the cylinder, the piston slowly sinks into the floor.

Electricity and Magnetism

What is electricity?

Electricity is a kind of energy. In order to understand how this energy is created, you have to know something about atoms. Atoms are the tiny, tiny bits of matter that all things are made of. Atoms are so small that you can't see them even with the most powerful microscope. Though atoms are so small, they are made of even smaller parts. Some of these parts are called electrons (ih-LECK-tronz). Electrons cause electricity.

When electrons move around among the atoms of matter, there is a current of electricity. In some materials, the electrons are loosely attached to the atoms. This makes it easy to break the electrons loose and have them move to other atoms. Electrons are loosely attached in all metals. That is why people use metal wires to carry electricity from one place to another. We say that these wires are good "conductors," or carriers, of electricity.

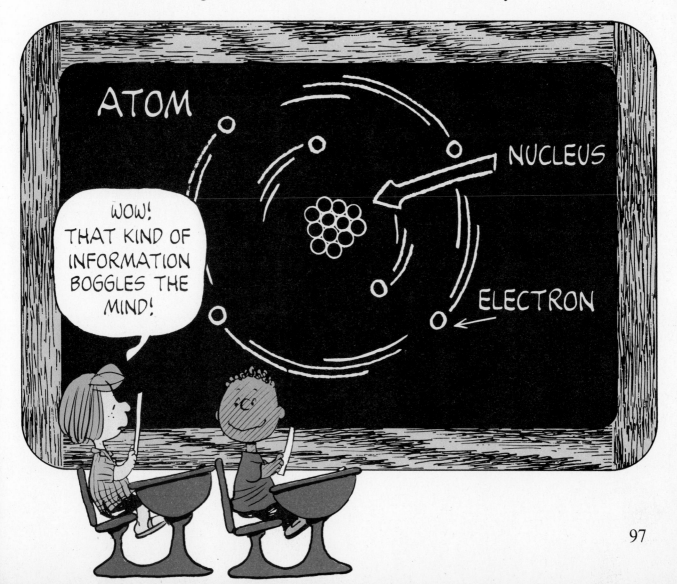

What is a magnet?

A magnet is something that can attract iron. A very simple magnet may be a bar of iron or steel. Sometimes the bar is bent into the form of a horseshoe.

A magnet's attraction is strongest at its ends, or poles. Every magnet has a north pole and a south pole. If you hold two magnets near each other, the north pole of one will be attracted to the south pole of the other. If you try to bring the north pole of one magnet together with the north pole of another, they will push apart, or repel, each other. This also happens with two south poles. Opposite poles attract each other. Poles of the same kind repel.

What do magnets have to do with electricity?

A lot. Magnetism and electricity are close relatives. In fact, electricity can produce magnetism. And magnetism can produce electricity.

A magnet has an invisible field, or cloud, of magnetic force around it. A wire with electricity running through it has the same kind of invisible magnetic field around it.

You can show the shape of a magnet's invisible field. Put a magnet under a piece of paper. Then sprinkle powdered iron on top of the paper.

Do some magnets run on electricity?

Yes. They are called electromagnets. You can make a small electromagnet by winding lots of thin copper wire around an iron nail. Use wire that has a protective covering. Scrape off about an inch of the covering at each end of the wire. Attach the ends to a battery, as in the picture. An electric current flows from the battery through the wire to the nail. And the nail becomes magnetic. It can pick up other iron things. If you disconnect the wire from the battery, the nail loses almost all of its magnetism.

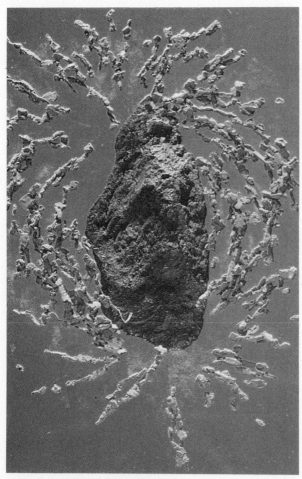

Colored iron filings show magnetic field around piece of magnetite

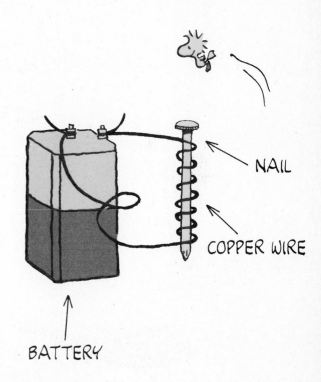

NAIL

COPPER WIRE

BATTERY

 The world's biggest magnet is 196 feet (59 meters) across and weighs 40,000 tons!

Are electromagnets better than ordinary magnets?

In at least one way, yes. An electromagnet works only when it is turned on. So with an electromagnet you can lift a heavy iron object and move it to any place you want. As soon as you shut off the electricity, the electromagnet will stop working. It will drop the iron at the place you choose.

You could not do this with an ordinary magnet. An ordinary magnet keeps holding on to iron things. That's why it is sometimes called a permanent magnet. "Permanent" means lasting forever. If you want to separate a piece of iron from a permanent magnet, you must pull it off.

How are electromagnets used?

Big electromagnets are often used in junkyards to load scrap iron into railroad cars. They are also used to separate iron from other kinds of scrap, such as aluminum or copper or glass. Small electromagnets are used to make some machines work. For example, a doorbell uses an electromagnet.

How does a doorbell work?

When you push the button outside a door, electricity goes through wires to a small electromagnet in the doorbell. The magnet pulls on a flat steel spring. The spring is attached to a little hammer that hits the bell. But as soon as the spring moves and the hammer hits the bell, the electric flow, or current, shuts off. This is because the spring's movement pulled apart two pieces of metal that were touching. The current can't flow unless these two pieces of metal touch each other. When the current stops, the spring bounces back to its original position. Now the two pieces of metal that were apart are touching each other again. So the current flows again. And the electromagnet pulls the spring to make the hammer strike the bell again. As long as you keep your finger on the button, the spring will keep flipping back and forth very fast. And the bell will keep on ringing.

A doorbell works by pushing a button — unless of course you have a door knocker. In that case you have a problem.

Sally Brown

BATTERY-OPERATED DOORBELL

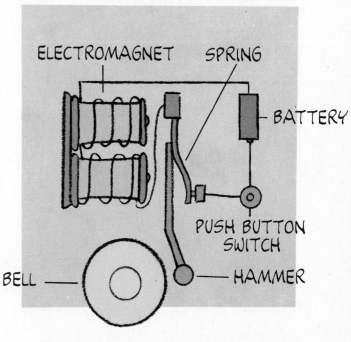

Where do electric currents come from?

Most of the electric currents that people use come from batteries or from machines called generators. The current that runs the lights, the toaster, the refrigerator, and other things in your house probably comes from a very large generator in a place called a power plant.

What is a generator?

A generator is a machine that makes electric current flow. A generator can be smaller than your big toe. Or it can be bigger than your living room. A small generator can power a bicycle's headlight. A large one can give power to a whole city.

How does a generator produce an electric current?

A generator changes one kind of energy into another. Every generator is run by something that turns or spins. The turning wheel of a bicycle runs the generator that powers its headlight. The spinning wheels or blades of a large engine run the generator that produces electric power for a city. In the generator, the spinning energy is turned into electric energy. Here's how.

The people who make generators keep certain scientific facts in mind:

1. Around every magnet are invisible lines of force.   2. If you move a coil of copper wire past a magnet, the wire cuts across the lines of force.
3. When the lines of force are cut by the wire, electricity flows through the wire.

Inside a generator are magnets (often electromagnets) and a coil of wire. The wire is usually around a rod called an armature (ARM-uh-choor). The engine that runs the generator moves the armature. As long as the armature keeps moving, the magnets' lines of force are cut. As long as the magnets' lines of force are cut, a current of electricity is produced, or generated.

What is a battery?

A battery is something that generates an electric current by chemical reaction. A chemical reaction may take place when chemicals mix together and change into other chemicals.

You've probably seen the battery that is inside a portable radio or a flashlight. It looks something like a small can. This can and everything inside it is called a dry cell. Some batteries are made up of one dry cell. Others use two or more. Inside dry cells are all the chemicals and other things needed to produce electric current.

The chemicals in dry cells are in the form of jellies or pastes. They can't be spilled. That's why these cells are called dry cells. There are also cells called wet cells. The chemicals inside these are liquids. Some batteries called storage batteries can be recharged and used over and over again. One kind of storage battery is used to start a car. It is made of three or six cells in a plastic box.

Most batteries come in standard sizes and shapes. Some tiny ones are used to run watches. Some huge ones are used to run submarines.

Batteries

The world's oldest working battery is in a laboratory in England. It has been generating a tiny current of electricity since 1840!

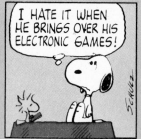

How does a battery produce an electric current?

Batteries produce currents by chemical reaction. Usually, a cell of a battery has three chemicals. One, called the electrolyte (ih-LECK-troe-lite), causes the other two to react. When the two chemicals react, the electrons in their atoms do a lot of moving around. One chemical ends up with a load of extra electrons. Another chemical ends up with a shortage of electrons. In this way, these two chemicals become what is called electrically charged. The chemical with extra electrons gets a negative or minus charge. The chemical with a shortage of electrons gets a positive or plus charge. When the chemicals are electrically charged, the electricity is ready to flow out of the battery.

In order for the flow to begin, there must be a complete path for the current to follow. Such a path is called an electric circuit (SIR-kit). The electrons move around the circuit by using energy given to them by the battery. Suppose the circuit is in a flashlight. As the electrons move along, they change electric energy to heat energy and light energy. And the bulb lights up.

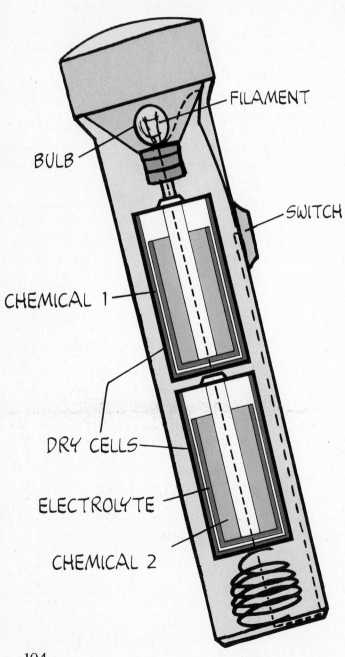

FILAMENT

BULB

SWITCH

CHEMICAL 1

DRY CELLS

ELECTROLYTE

CHEMICAL 2

What makes batteries go dead?

When a battery can no longer produce current, we say it is dead. A battery stops producing all current when its chemical reaction stops. The reaction stops when some of the chemicals have been used up. That means the chemicals have changed into other chemicals.

Can a dead or weak battery be made to work like new again?

Ordinary flashlight batteries can't be renewed, but certain other batteries can. These are called storage batteries. Renewing a battery is called recharging it. Cars have rechargeable batteries. Some electric drills, small vacuum cleaners, and electronic calculators run on rechargeable batteries.

How are car batteries recharged?

Car batteries recharge automatically when the car's engine is running. The engine is connected to a generator. The generator forces a current to run backward through the battery. This means the new chemicals change back into the old chemicals. The chemicals can react again to generate more electricity. Recharging is what allows the battery to keep starting the car every day for years.

What is an electric shock?

An electric shock is what you feel when electricity passes through your body. A strong shock can kill a person or cause painful burns. A fairly weak shock can sting your skin and make your muscles jerk.

Shocks are no fun. So here are a few "nevers" to remember. Never touch electrical things if they are wet, or if your hands are wet. And don't touch them if you are standing in a puddle or a bathtub. Water is a good conductor of electricity, so wetness increases your chances of getting a bad shock. Never climb telephone poles. And always keep away from any place that has a sign saying "Danger. High Voltage." This doesn't mean you should be afraid of electrical things. Just be very, very careful with them.

What is a power plant?

A power plant is a place where large amounts of electrical energy are generated.

There are at least seven different kinds of power plants. All of them have generators. But the power to run the generators comes from different things —steam, water, gas, or even wind.

The three most common kinds of plants are steam-turbine plants, hydro-electric (HY-droe-ih-LECK-tric) plants, and atomic or nuclear (NOO-klee-ur) plants.

How does a steam-turbine plant generate electricity?

A steam-turbine plant uses steam to spin the wheels of a turbine. The spinning motion of the turbine runs the generator that produces the electric current.

Steam is made by burning oil, coal, or gas to boil water. A huge amount of water is boiled. It makes a huge amount of steam. A steam-run plant is like a giant tea kettle with steam blowing out the spout. But instead of going through a spout, the steam goes through a tunnel. Inside the tunnel are wheels with blades. This tunnel full of blades is the turbine.

When steam blows through the tunnel, it makes the blades spin very fast. When the blades spin, the rod they are mounted on spins also. The rod is connected to the electric generators. When the rod spins, the generators run and produce electric currents.

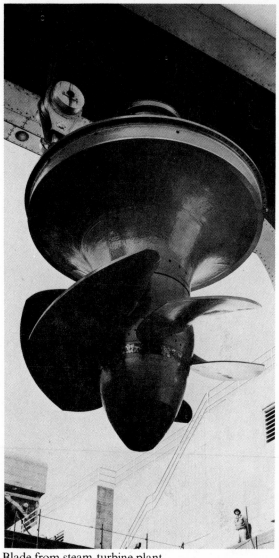
Blade from steam-turbine plant

How does a hydroelectric power plant generate electricity?

A hydroelectric power plant uses a water-powered turbine to run a generator. The water comes from a reservoir (REZ-ur-vwar) or a lake. Most of it is held back by a large wall called a dam. Gravity, the force that pulls everything downward, makes some water flow through tunnels from the top of the dam to the bottom. Just before the water is let out at the bottom of the dam, it runs through the turbines and makes them turn. Flowing water can turn turbines just as wind can turn windmills or pinwheels. When turbines turn, they make the generators turn, and electric currents are produced.

The world's largest power plant can make enough electrical energy to turn on 60 million 100-watt light bulbs.

107

What is a watt?

A watt is the unit used to measure electric power. A 100-watt light bulb uses 100 units of electrical energy every second. A 60-watt light bulb uses only 60 units of electrical energy every second. In either case, electrical energy is changed into heat and light energy. The watt is named after James Watt, the man who invented the steam engine.

How does an atomic power plant generate electricity?

An atomic power plant works almost the same as a steam-turbine power plant does. But an atomic plant doesn't burn coal, oil, or gas. Instead, it uses the metal uranium (you-RAY-nee-um) to make heat for boiling water. Instead of burning the uranium in a furnace, the uranium is put in a nuclear reactor. There, the atoms that make up the uranium split. And they produce huge amounts of nuclear energy. In doing this, a great amount of heat is given off. The heat turns water to steam. The steam blows through turbines, and the turbines turn the generators.

How does an electric current go from a power plant to people's houses?

It leaves the power plant through thick, heavy wires called transmission (tranz-MISH-un) lines. The current is sent out under high electrical pressure, or at high "voltage." The lines are held up off the ground by tall metal towers.

Transmission lines stretch for miles. When they come to a town where people need electricity, some of the lines go into a place called a substation. The substation changes the high-voltage electricity into low-voltage electricity, which is safer. The low-voltage electricity then goes through wires from the substation to a transformer. This makes the voltage even lower. From there it travels to houses, factories, and offices. In big cities, the wires carrying electricity to customers are in pipes or tunnels under the streets. In small towns, the wires are strung between wooden poles.

! The same person, Michael Faraday, invented the electric motor, the generator, and the transformer! !

109

What is a brownout?

Sometimes the area around a power plant needs more power than usual. This often happens in the summer when people are using air conditioners. Sometimes one power district can buy power from a neighboring power district. Special cables are set up to make this possible.

If your power district cannot buy enough from a neighbor, it may send out power to your home at lower voltage. This is called a brownout.

If the voltage is reduced just a little, you won't notice it. But if it is reduced 5 percent or more, your lights will be dimmer. And some appliances, such as your toaster and your iron, won't work as well as usual.

What is a blackout?

When the power plant stops sending electricity to your neighborhood, you have a blackout. The power company may do this purposely, in order to send more power to other areas during a shortage. Or, if something goes wrong at the power plant, there may be a blackout that nobody wants in a large area.

During a blackout, your street would be completely dark at night. You couldn't watch TV or listen to the radio or stereo (unless yours run on batteries). Your refrigerator would stop working. If you have an electric stove, your parents couldn't cook. You would have to do your homework by candlelight or flashlight!

WAM! WAM! WAM!

I REFUSE TO STAY OUT IN A BLACKOUT— IT'S A GOOD WAY TO GET MUGGED

What is an electric motor?

An electric motor is a kind of machine that is powered by electricity. The motor changes electric energy into movement that can do work. For example, an electric blender has a small motor inside it. When the blender is plugged in and the motor switch turned on, the motor starts to spin. It causes the blades inside the blender's large container to spin, too. The blades then can cut up any food you put in the container.

112

Why are electric wires covered with plastic or rubber?

The plastic or rubber insulates (IN-suh-lates) the wire. This means it keeps the electricity from leaking out through the sides of the wire. An insulated wire is safe to touch. A bare wire could shock or even kill someone who touches it. Sometimes when a wire is old, the insulation becomes cracked and starts to peel or break off. When this happens, someone might easily get a shock, or a fire might start. If you see a wire with cracked insulation, you should tell a grownup so that the wire can be replaced with a new one.

What makes a light go on when you flip a switch?

When you flip on a switch, you complete an electric circuit (SIR-kit). A circuit is like a closed loop. When electrons travel along a circuit, they eventually go back to the place where they started—as if they were going around in a circle. As long as the electrons keep flowing, the bulb stays lit. If you break the circuit, by cutting the wire or turning off the switch, the flow of electrons stops. Then the light goes out.

Open circuit

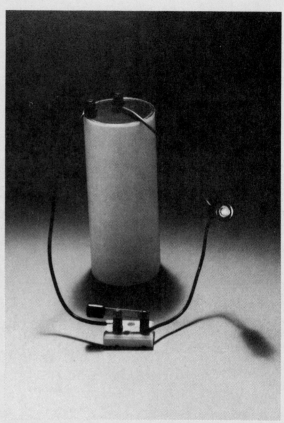

Closed circuit   Light bulb on

114

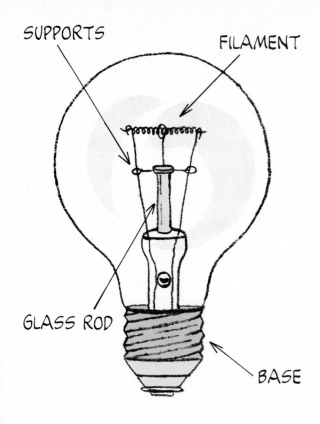

SUPPORTS

FILAMENT

GLASS ROD

BASE

What makes a light bulb light up?

Inside a light bulb is a thin wire called a filament (FILL-uh-munt). When electricity passes through the filament, the filament becomes very hot. It becomes so hot that it glows and gives off a bright white light. The glass part of a light bulb keeps air from reaching the filament. It is important to keep air away from the filament because air has oxygen (OCK-suh-jin) in it. Oxygen is one of the three things needed to start a fire. The other two are heat and something that can burn. A white-hot filament has the heat and is burnable. If any oxygen happened to reach a hot filament, it would burn up in an instant.

What makes light bulbs burn out?

When a light bulb stops working, we say that it has "burned" out. But it didn't really burn. What really happened was that the bulb's filament broke. When the filament breaks, electrons can't pass through it. When electrons can't pass through the filament, then the filament can't get white-hot and glow.

Heat is what makes the filament break. Heat causes tiny cracks to form in the filament. The more you use the bulb, the bigger the cracks become. Finally, one of the cracks will stretch all the way through the filament, and the filament will break apart.

SOME OF US CAN'T SLEEP WITHOUT A NIGHT LIGHT!

115

Who invented the electric light bulb?

Thomas Edison in 1879. He was one of the greatest inventors who ever lived. If you ask people to name some important inventors, usually the first one they will think of is Edison. His most famous inventions were the phonograph, the electric light bulb, and a motion-picture machine called a kinetoscope (kih-NEE-tuh-scope). All together he and his helpers invented over 1,000 things.

Thomas Alva Edison

 The oldest working light bulb has been burning in a firehouse in California since 1901!

What is the difference between a light bulb and a fluorescent lamp?

The most obvious difference is their shape. A light bulb usually has a pear shape. A fluorescent (flow-RESS-unt) lamp usually has a tube shape. But that is not all.

In a light bulb, light is made with a glowing hot filament. But in a fluorescent lamp, the glow comes from a special white coating on the inside of the glass tube. The coating glows whenever certain invisible rays, called ultraviolet (UL-truh-VYE-uh-lit) rays, hit it. These ultraviolet rays are made when you turn on the electricity. When the lamp is on, electrons shoot from one end of the tube to the other. The tube is filled with a special gas that gives off ultraviolet rays whenever electrons shoot through it. Fluorescent lamps help save money because they use much less electric power than light bulbs do.

116

What makes flash bulbs flash?

Oxygen. Flash bulbs have oxygen sealed inside. When you press the button on your camera, electric current flows through the bulb's filament. The filament glows. But the glow doesn't last the way it does in an ordinary light bulb. That is because the oxygen makes the filament burn up in a flash of bright light. This flash gives you a lot of light in enough time to snap a picture.

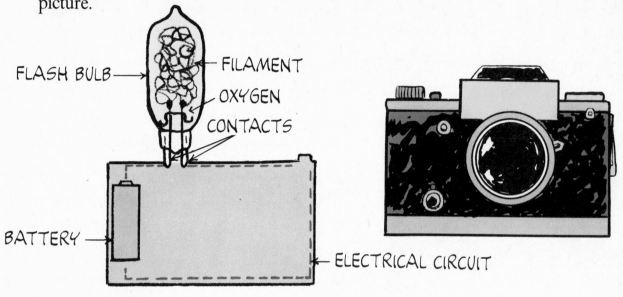

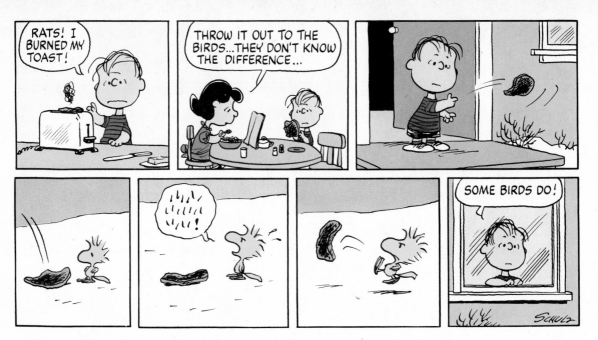

What makes toasters and electric irons get hot?

When a toaster or electric iron is turned on, an electric current flows through a coil of wire. This means that electrons are moving along among the atoms that make up the coil of the toaster or iron. As the electrons make their way, they bump into atoms. This bumping changes the energy of the current into heat energy. The coil becomes hot.

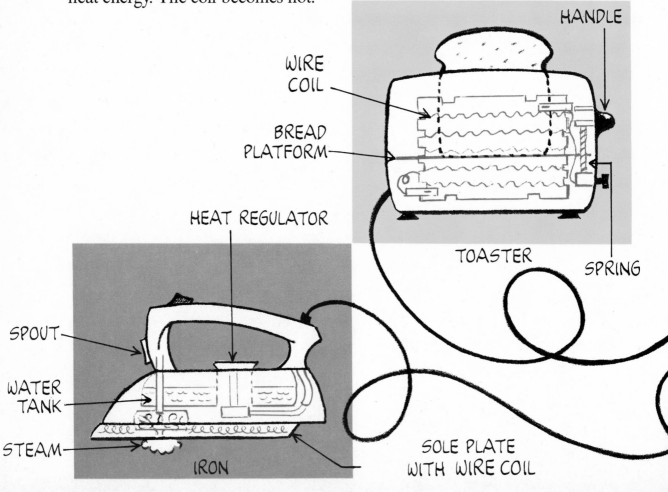

What does a fuse do?

It protects your house from fires caused by electricity. All electric current that comes into your house must pass through the fuse. If you take the fuse out, the circuit is broken. No electricity comes in. If you put the fuse back, your house has current again.

Inside the fuse is a piece of metal. If this piece of metal gets too hot, it melts very quickly. Melting is the way it protects your house.

For example, suppose you are using an air conditioner, a TV, an iron, and three lamps. Then you put on the toaster. You are now causing too much current to go through the circuit in your house. The wires become very hot and they could start a fire. However, before this can happen, the metal piece in the fuse melts from the heat. We say the fuse blew. Electrons can no longer flow through the wires of your house. So an electrical fire will not start.

In order to get electric current flowing into your house again, you must put in a new fuse. But first you have to shut off at least one appliance, such as the toaster or the iron. Then less current will be flowing through the wires in your house. The smaller current can be safely carried without blowing the fuse.

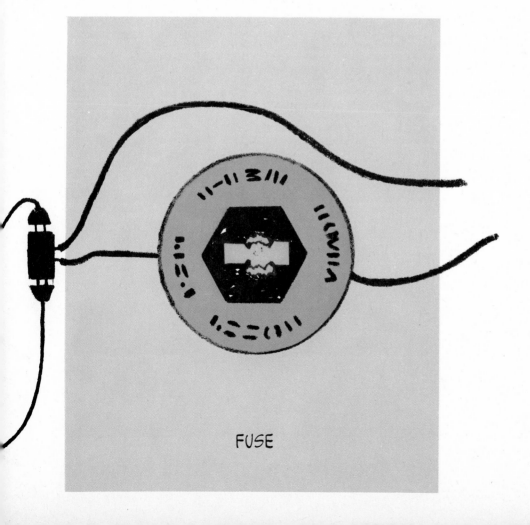

FUSE

Do circuits in all buildings have fuses?

No. Fuses are becoming old-fashioned. Newer buildings have circuit breakers instead. On the outside, circuit breakers look like ordinary light switches. But on the inside, a circuit breaker has a spring that bends when it gets hot. The spring will get hot if too much current is going through the circuit. If the spring gets hot and bends, the circuit breaker will flip to the off position. The current shuts off. After you wait a few minutes for the spring to cool, you can flip the circuit breaker back on. But before you do that, you should turn off some of your lights and appliances. Then the circuit breaker probably won't switch off again.

How does the electric company know how much to charge each customer?

Each customer's house or apartment has a meter that measures how much electric energy the customer uses. The numbers on the dial tell the company's meter reader how many kilowatt-hours of electrical energy the customer has used. A kilowatt is a unit of electric power. One kilowatt is equal to 1,000 watts. If you use a 1,000-watt iron for an hour, then you have used one kilowatt-hour of electricity. If you keep a 100-watt bulb burning for ten hours, that also adds up to one kilowatt-hour. The meter keeps track of every little bit of electrical energy that is used. And it all adds up to a certain number of kilowatt-hours.

Can electricity help people send messages?

Yes. If you want to contact someone far away, and you want to do it quickly, you must use a telegraph, a telephone, a radio, or maybe a television. All these methods use electrical energy.

What is a telegraph?

A telegraph is the oldest method of using electricity to send and receive messages. Samuel F. B. Morse invented the telegraph in 1837. For the first time people could contact each other instantly between any two places that could be connected by wires. Before the telegraph, messages had to be sent by mail or by private messenger. The telegraph is no longer used much. It has been replaced by telephones and radios.

How does a telegraph work?

Besides wires and batteries, a telegraph system has two main parts. One is a sender, called a key. The other is a receiver, called a sounder. The person working the telegraph is called the operator.

The key is really just a switch. The operator presses the key to make current flow through the wires. When the operator stops pressing, the current stops. The sounder has an electromagnet. When the current is on, the electromagnet moves a lever made of iron. When the lever moves, it goes "tap" or "click" against another piece of iron. Different patterns of clicks stand for different letters of the alphabet. The receiving operator listens to the clicks and can understand the message that the sending operator is spelling. This system of using clicks to stand for letters is called Morse code.

Samuel F. B. Morse sends the first telegram

Do people still use Morse code?

Not usually. But a code much like Morse's is still used by radio operators. Instead of clicks, the radio code uses short and long beeps, called dots and dashes. If you know someone who operates a radio as a hobby, maybe you can listen to people talking to each other in code. If you learn the code, you will be able to understand what they are saying.

Write your name here, using Morse code.

Can you read this?

Was there any fast way to send messages between America and Europe before telephones were invented?

Yes. In 1866 a heavy wire called a cable was laid across the bottom of the Atlantic Ocean. This cable made it possible for people to send telegraph messages between America and Europe. Before the cable was laid, messages had to go by ship. This meant that people didn't know what was happening on the other side of the ocean until days or weeks later.

Now there are cables under all the world's oceans. They carry telephone messages and other electric signals.

 The longest undersea cable runs about 9,000 miles (more than 14,000 kilometers), from Australia to Canada!

Cable on ocean floor

THAT'S TOO DEEP FOR ME.

GOOD GRIEF!

How does a telephone work?

Every time you talk, you start sound waves moving through the air. When you talk over the telephone to a friend, the sound waves from your voice enter the part of the phone called the mouthpiece. The sound waves flow against a paper-thin piece of metal called a diaphragm (DYE-uh-fram). They make it vibrate—move back and forth very quickly.

As the diaphragm vibrates, it jiggles tiny bits of carbon in a small box attached to it. The carbon bits bunch together or spread apart in time with the vibrations of your voice.

An electric current flows over the telephone wires between your house and your friend's house. The action of the carbon bits changes the strength of the electric current that goes over the wires. The current is strong when the carbon bits bunch together. It is weak when they spread apart. As a result, the spurts of current follow the same pattern as the sound waves from your voice.

When the spurts of current reach your friend's house, they must be changed back into the sound of your voice. In your friend's phone (and in yours too) is a small electromagnet. When the spurts of current reach the electromagnet, another thin metal diaphragm begins to vibrate. This diaphragm is in the part of the phone called the earpiece. The vibrations set sound waves in motion. The sound waves reach your friend's ears, and your friend hears you say "Hello!"

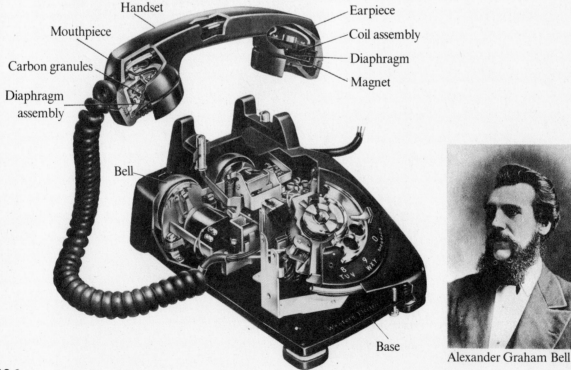

Handset · Mouthpiece · Carbon granules · Diaphragm assembly · Bell · Earpiece · Coil assembly · Diaphragm · Magnet · Base

Alexander Graham Bell

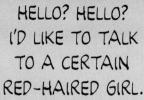
HELLO? HELLO? I'D LIKE TO TALK TO A CERTAIN RED-HAIRED GIRL.

 There are about 400 million telephones in the world! More than a third of them are in the United States!

HI, CHUCK? IT'S PEPPERMINT PATTY. YOU DIALED THE WRONG NUMBER... BUT THAT'S O.K.

 The average American makes about 1,000 telephone calls each year!

WILL YOU TWO GET OFF THE PHONE? THIS IS A PARTY LINE AND I'M STILL TALKING!

 Alexander Graham Bell invented the telephone while trying (without success) to invent a hearing aid for deaf people!

A PARTY... DID SHE SAY A PARTY? I'LL BE RIGHT OVER.

How does a radio work?

Radio is a way of sending voices and music through the air instead of along electric wires. It's like a wireless telephone. In fact, when radio was first invented, people called it the wireless. Instead of wires, radio uses electromagnetic waves. These waves can travel through air—and even through space.

How are radio waves made?

Radio waves are made by a transmitter with the help of an antenna. A transmitter is a radio sender. The set you listen to is a radio receiver. The radio programs you hear are sent out by transmitters from radio-broadcasting studios.

A transmitter makes an electric current that vibrates very fast. It vibrates many thousands or even millions of times a second. Such a fast vibrating current can flow through a wire like an ordinary current. But when it is sent through an antenna, it changes form. Out of the antenna comes an invisible electromagnetic field that reaches for miles. Sometimes it even reaches halfway around the earth. This field is made of radio waves. These waves can be picked up by a receiver.

What does an antenna look like?

An antenna can be a piece of wire. Or it may be a whole bunch of wires hanging like a net from tall towers. Sometimes an antenna may be a metal pole or rod sticking straight up. Other times it may be shaped like a dish. The type of antenna used depends on how fast the radio waves are vibrating, how far you want them to go, and in which direction you want them to go.

How do radio waves carry voices and music?

If you went into a radio station, you would see someone talking into a microphone or playing music on a phonograph. A microphone is much like the mouthpiece of a telephone. When you talk into it, sound waves cause a piece of metal in the microphone to vibrate. An electric current flows through the microphone. The current vibrates in time with the vibrations of voices or music. This current can travel only along wires. But the job of a radio station is to send this current out to radio receivers. The trick, then, is to get the microphone current to hitch a piggyback ride on the transmitter current. The combination can travel through the air or space as radio waves.

A radio transmitter has a part called a modulator (MOJ-uh-lay-tur). It mixes the microphone current with the transmitter current. In this way, the microphone vibrations can leave the antenna together with the transmitter's radio waves. That is how the sounds can be made to travel out through air and space.

Radio waves travel at about the same speed as light (186,000 miles or 297,600 kilometers per second). There is nothing faster!

Can radio waves be sent in a straight beam?

Yes. Most antennas send out radio waves in all directions. To send the waves in a straight beam, you need a special antenna. This type of antenna is curved, like a dish. Radio waves come out in all directions from a rod pointing from the middle of the dish. Many of these waves then hit the curved part of the dish. The curve causes the waves to bounce back out away from the dish. Then they travel in a straight beam.

Can a dish-shaped antenna receive radio waves?

Yes. Like most antennas, dish-shaped antennas can receive as well as send. Some, like radar antennas, send and receive at the same time. Dish antennas are very good for communicating with space satellites. They can be aimed directly at a satellite, so that a clear, strong signal can be sent thousands of miles away. When receiving, a dish antenna picks up signals only from the direction in which it is aimed. The signal comes through very clearly.

Dish-shaped antenna

Who invented the radio?

Guglielmo (goo-lee-YELL-moh) Marconi (mar-KOE-nee) invented radio in 1895 when he was 21 years old. Marconi became very interested in science when he was a boy. He began doing experiments when he was 16. For a long time, scientists had said it should be possible to make a radio—or wireless telegraph, as it was called. But nobody could figure out how to do it. Marconi studied the other scientists' ideas and experiments. Then, when he was 20, he tried to invent a radio on his own. Finally he built a transmitter and a receiver. The transmitter could send telegraph messages across his attic without wires. But would it work over a long distance?

Marconi had his brother carry the receiver over a hill, far away out of sight. The brother also carried a rifle. Then Marconi used the transmitter to send a message to his brother. Marconi stopped and listened. Bang! He heard a rifle shot in the distance. It was his brother's signal that the message had been received. Marconi's invention was a success.

EXHIBITION OF INVENTORS

TODAY'S LECTURE STARTS AT 2 P.M. ON G. MARCONI

Early radio makers broadcast their own programs. If they hadn't, no one would have had a reason to buy a radio. There were no other programs to listen to!

How many radio-broadcasting stations are there?

The United States has about 8,000 radio-broadcasting stations.

Why don't the radio waves from different stations get mixed up in the air?

When you play your radio, you turn the dial to a number. The number may be 700 or 1100 or one of many other numbers. (There may be just a 7 or an 11 on your radio dial. If the radio is small, the zeros will be left out.) Each number stands for what is called a frequency (FREE-kwun-see). Each station broadcasts at a different frequency. The frequency is the rate of vibration of the waves that come from the station's transmitter. Your radio can "tune in" on the particular frequency you want to hear. Waves from other stations go by without being picked up.

 About half the radios in the world are in the United States!

What is a two-way radio?

A two-way radio is one that can send out radio signals and pick them up also. The radio you have in your house is a one-way radio. It only receives radio waves. The radio transmitter in a broadcasting station is also a one-way radio. It sends out radio waves.

A two-way radio is the kind you sometimes see taxicab drivers using. They talk into it to tell the cab company where they are taking you. They also get messages from the cab company through this radio.

People use two-way radios in boats, airplanes, police cars, and other places where it's not possible to have telephone wires.

135

What is a radio ham?

A radio ham has nothing to do with food. It is a person who sends and receives radio messages as a hobby. Many boys and girls become radio hams. They send messages to other hams by code or by voice. There are special frequencies set aside for them to use. In order to send messages, hams have to pass a test and get a license. They also must have special equipment—a transmitter, a receiver, and an antenna. Many hams build their own equipment from kits. If you want to become a ham, the equipment will cost you anywhere from fifty dollars to many thousands of dollars.

What is a CB radio?

CB stands for Citizens Band. It is a group of frequencies that is reserved for ordinary people to use. You do not need a license to use a CB radio. Usually, people have CB radios in their cars. Truck drivers use CB's a lot. They talk with other drivers and find out about traffic conditions.

A special language has grown up among CB users. It is a kind of code. For example, "Smoky" means policeman. "Rolling double nickels" means driving at 55 miles an hour.

137

How does black-and-white television work?

The screen that you look at is the front end of something called a picture tube. The screen is coated on the inside with a chemical that glows when it is hit by electrons. The electrons come from a part of the TV called an electron gun. It is in the back of the picture tube. If you look closely at the screen, you can see lots of thin lines running across it. The electron gun fires a row of electrons along each line. Some places on the line are hit by a lot of electrons, and they light up brightly. Other places are hit by fewer electrons. These places appear light gray, dark gray, or black. The darkness depends on how many electrons hit them. When you look at all the light and dark spots together, your eyes see a picture. It's like a black-and-white photograph in a newspaper. If you look closely at a newspaper photograph, you can see that it is made up of lots of tiny dots.

138

How does a picture get to your television set?

A picture gets to your TV in much the same way that sound reaches your radio. Radio waves carry the picture from a transmitting station, through the air, to your TV set.

How is it possible to see color on a TV?

Color television is very much like a comic strip or a color photograph printed in a magazine. The picture is a mixture of thousands and thousands of little colored dots (red, green, and blue). If you look at a color television screen very closely, you can see the little dots. When the set is off, the dots look gray or silvery. But when the set is on, the dots light up.

The dots are made of a chemical that glows when hit by a beam of electrons shot from an electron gun. A black-and-white television set has only one electron gun. But a color set has three, one for each color—red, green, and blue. Other colors—yellow, orange, purple, brown, black, or white—are made to appear on the screen by controlling how many red, green, and blue dots light up. For example, a picture of a glass of orange juice would be made of a large number of red dots and a smaller number of green dots. The tiny red, green, and blue dots mix together to form many colors.

A color television camera separates everything it looks at into red, green, or blue. Then, the television station transmits a red picture, a green picture, and a blue picture. The television set catches these pictures with its antenna and sends the pictures to the three electron guns. The three pictures are mixed on the screen to show the same colors as the camera saw.

Here you see how a magnet can make electrons move. The television screen has a black spot and a crooked picture because magnetism is bending the beams of electrons that shoot from the electron gun to the screen.

141

How does a phonograph record make sounds?

The surface of a record is covered with narrow circles that are very close together. If you look at those circles with a magnifying glass or a microscope, you will see that they are very wavy. When the record turns, the waves make the stylus—the phonograph needle—vibrate. The vibrations in the stylus cause vibrations in the strength of an electric current. The current goes to something called an amplifier. It makes the current stronger. Then, current from the amplifier makes a loudspeaker vibrate. And you hear the sound that was recorded.

What is a phonograph?

"Phonograph" is a word that is becoming very old-fashioned. People once used it to mean a record player or a hi-fi set. A modern phonograph is usually called a stereo.

What is hi-fi?

Hi-fi is short for high fidelity. Fidelity refers to how accurately a record or stereo set makes sounds. A high-fidelity recording of an orchestra should sound almost exactly like a real orchestra.

What does stereo mean?

Stereo means a sound-recording system that uses two or more microphones for recording and two or more loudspeakers for listening. The extra microphones and loudspeakers make the sound more realistic. With a stereo system, different sounds come from different loudspeakers. For example, you might hear a saxophone on one speaker and a guitar on the other. It would be just like having the musicians right in the same room with you. On a nonstereo phonograph, the guitar and saxophone sounds would be mixed together and come out of one speaker. Another word for nonstereo is monaural (mon-OR-ul), which means "one ear." Listening to a monaural record is almost like listening to live music with only one of your ears.

How does a tape recorder work?

A tape recorder works by magnetism. The tape is a plastic ribbon coated with a chemical called iron oxide. Each tiny bit, or particle, of iron oxide is like a little magnet.

Inside a tape recorder is an electromagnet called a recording head. When electric waves from a microphone go into the tape recorder, they cause vibrations in the field around the electromagnet. As the tape passes through the electromagnet's field, the bits of iron oxide on the tape are magnetized into different patterns.

When you play back the tape, the patterns on it affect another electromagnet called a playback head. This electromagnet makes waves that go into an amplifier. The amplifier makes the waves stronger. The strong waves make a loudspeaker vibrate. The sound vibrations that come from the speaker are just like the ones that went into the microphone.

Index

References to pictures are in *italic type*.

weather forecasting, 85
weighing, 18–19
wet cell battery, 103
wheel, 4
    steering, 12, *12*
Whitney, Eli, 46, *46*, 47
windup watch, 21
wire, electric, 109, 113
"wireless," *see* radio

woodwind instruments, 55
wristwatch, *see* watch

x-rays, 64
   tube, *64*
xylophone, 50

zipper, 44–45, *44–45*